GOD IS NOT DONE WITH THE NORTH AMERICAN CHURCH

From Dying to Dangerous

A Radical New Pathway for Churches to Reignite Kingdom Culture

GARY SMITH

Thank You!

I'd like to thank the following:

The Father, Son and Holy Spirit.
All praise and thankfulness goes first to them.

I'd like to thank my amazing wife and my awesome kids and their excellent choices in spouses. You are a huge part of the stories in this book and I treasure you all. I am deeply grateful for the influence of Harold Bullok in my life. There is literally not a day that goes by that I am not considering something you have taught me.

I am thankful for Trevor Skalberg and his faith to cast a vision that seemed impossible. I am also deeply thankful for these faithful men who invested deeply in my life: Pastor Lynne Smith, Church Planter Andy Williams, Robert Buck (pastor, leader, and faithful friend from the Swampy Cree in MB, CA), Nate Vedoya, and Rob Blackaby. Each of you have had a deep impact in my transformation into Christ-likeness.

I am grateful for the leaders in Canada who cast a massive vision for Canada that captivated my heart and my life for over 20 years and that allowed me to plant churches with leaders from sea to sea in Canada and amongst the multiple nations and language groups of Canada. I want to thank Peaceful Profits for helping this book to become a reality.

Table of Contents

Introduction

Jesus said, "I Will Build My Church."
–Matthew 16:18

D ear Reader:

The Church does not have to die…

In the last seven days, an average of 135 churches closed their doors in the United States.[1] Permanently.

And while an average of 73 new churches were birthed in the same time span, unfortunately, 35% of them will not be open 5 years from now[2].

That math represents a harsh reality. The US population is growing by approximately 3 million annually, and we, the collective Church, are rapidly losing ground. We are called, as Jesus tells us in the Great Commission, to "go therefore and make disciples of all the nations, baptizing them in the name of the Father and the Son and the Holy Spirit, teaching them to observe all that I commanded you" (Matthew 28:19-20).

---

1   Thom S. Rainer, "Your Church is Going to Die," New Churches, accessed November 30, 2025, https://www.newchurches.com/article/your-church-is-going-to-die/.

2 ibid.

Our assignment, as believers in Jesus, is to increase the harvest, to bring in more souls into the Kingdom of God. And yet, our church attendance numbers are dwindling at a rapid pace.

I love Jesus and I love His people, and I believe you do too. I love people who do not know him yet, and I hope that you do as well. And I love you—the faithful ones called to serve His people.

It is out of this love and out of my experiences walking with God and working with hundreds of church planters, pastors and churches, that I have designed this book. It will be your guide and roadmap so you can walk into the amazing, ripe North American harvest field, with courage, hope, and a steadfast determination to change the tide of the dying church.

Throughout this book, I will show you how to use the Church Planting Pathway to start a new church or to increase the number of attendees in an existing church through building relationships with new believers first.

For the past three decades, I have served diligently alongside church planters, missionaries, pastors, and Christ followers, who have allowed their hearts to be broken for the sake of their lost communities. While I have served alongside ministries in North America, Africa, and Cuba for over 30 years, I've only recently been given the freedom to compile everything I've learned from these great men and women of God. With that information, I developed my signature program, the Church Planting Pathway, which is transforming how new churches are planted and affecting the eternal destinies in unreached places for Christ.

Even if you don't yet feel called to plant a new church or ministry, within these pages you will find a wealth of ideas and information to strengthen your existing ministries and develop more effective methods for evangelism and disciple-making.

I have talked with Godly men and women from every walk of life, every area of ministry—from thriving rural churches, bursting at their seams, to urban cathedrals with a mere twelve members, to bustling immigrant congregations, to tiny country churches deep in the heart of flyover country. Each one, regardless of their location, has told me the same thing: "Planting a church is so hard!"

In the American south, they say, "People have heard it too much." In the north, they say, "People haven't heard the Gospel in years." In Quebec, they say, "People curse the church here." The overwhelming belief is that people are not open to the Gospel and people in all of these places say…

It is too hard.

And on the surface, it *does* seem hard…

In the last two decades alone, US church attendance has dropped 12% according to Gallup[3]. In Canada, one third of church buildings will be gone in the next decade![4]

---

3   Jeffrey M. Jones, "U.S. Church Membership Down Sharply in Past Two Decades," Gallup, April 18, 2019, https://news.gallup.com/poll/248837/church-membership-down-sharply-past-two-decades.aspx.

4   National Trust for Canada, "Canada is Losing Its Churches: Can Communities Afford to Let That Happen?" Broadview, July 24, 2025, https://broadview.org/cui-report-church-closures/.

Especially post-COVID, church attendance in most denominations is at record lows.[5] It's gotten so bad that, in recent years, foreign nations have begun sending evangelists to the US and Canada in greater numbers than we Westerners are commissioning missionaries to travel to the uttermost parts of the earth.[6]

Stop and consider…How do these stats hit you? Go back and read them again…slowly…

Back when the Apostle Paul was planting churches, the majority of those he birthed were within modern-day Turkey. Now, there's virtually no Christianity left there, less than three percent.[7] Is North America headed down a similar pathway?

Does The Church In North America *Have* to Die?

In my opinion, the answer is No! What do you think?

Rarely do we hear about this dying church. No one seems to be talking much about how dire the situation actually is. Do *you* feel concerned?

Mark Twain famously said, "The report of my death was an exaggeration." I think we need to say, "News of the dying North American church is going radically *under*exaggerated!"

---

5   Jeffrey M. Jones, "Church Attendance Has Declined in Most U.S. Religious Groups," Gallup, March 25, 2024, https://news.gallup.com/poll/642548/church-attendance-declined-religious-groups.aspx.

6   "Missionaries from the Global South Try to Save the Godless West," The Economist, January 12, 2019, https://www.economist.com/international/2019/01/12/missionaries-from-the-global-south-try-to-save-the-godless-west.

7 "2022 Report on International Religious Freedom: Turkey (Türkiye)," US Department of State, 2022, https://www.state.gov/reports/2022-report-on-international-religious-freedom/turkey/.

Over the last twenty years, I've helped hundreds of pastors and church planters to creatively accomplish new ways of doing a very old thing—introducing the lost and broken to a Savior who loves them passionately.

Throughout this book, I want to accomplish a few things with you:

1. I want to awaken you to the real situation, offering both a clarion call and a framework to provide you solutions to the most pressing of our collective problems.

2. I want to introduce you to some of my friends—amazing men and women who are wholeheartedly chasing after Jesus, loving their communities, and seeing great life transformations and thriving churches.

3. And, lastly, I want to encourage you to run your race with endurance and joy, as you awaken to the ripe harvest fields that Jesus is inviting you into (John 4).

This book is my best effort to provide you, Pastor, Christ-follower, passionate Church Planter, with the tools you need to see an aggressive shift. Consider this book the defibrillator paddles we will need to help awaken and revitalize our collective efforts to fulfill the Great Commission in North America and beyond.

Jesus promised that He would build a Church that would prevail against the Kingdom of

Darkness (Matthew 16:8). Has He failed? Has He quit? Has He given up? Of course not!!!

Then let us, together, understand the times and know what we should do (1 Chronicles 12:32).

I pray God's Spirit will use this book to awaken you to *a new perspective.* I believe Jesus longs to do EXTRAordinary things through you, and through His church.

If you want to learn more about how my team and I can help you accomplish more in your community, here's a QR code to chat with us. We look forward to hearing from you!

For an awakened Church,
Gary Smith

Would Anyone Miss Your Church?

Chapter 1

Who Cares?

"Like sheep without a shepherd."
–Matthew 9:36

There is a lot of *decay* throughout our churches that needs to be removed and replaced with dramatic strategic shifts if we are to be effective once again in fulfilling our assignment: the Great Commission.

Like root rot on an otherwise healthy tree, we need to uncover the realities of our situation so we can bring about the best solutions.

And while root rot is a helpful picture, it is not even a strong enough analogy for the dying that has been taking place in the modern Western church.

If Our Church Wasn't Here Tomorrow, Who Would Care?

In the last church I pastored before joining the Christian and Missionary Alliance as the Church Planting Director for New

England, I vividly recall a staff meeting that utterly remade the way I view what a church can be in its community…

It started out as a typical staff meeting at Bow Valley Baptist Church in Cochrane, Alberta, Canada. Discussions surrounded ways in which our church could reach out to the community. Then our Children's minister, Debbie, asked the most remarkable question—"If our church wasn't here tomorrow, would anyone notice? Who would care?"

A blanket of silence descended on the room. A holy hush for a moment which led immediately into a time of deep discussion and prayer around that very question.

Eventually, what was birthed out of that staff meeting became our new initiative: **LOVE Cochrane**, not so much a program as a way of thinking about how we would want our church to be viewed by the community. Greater still, it was a way of thinking about how we would want people in our community to view Jesus.

From that meeting, and after much discussion with the staff and our congregation, our mission statement became: *Love like Jesus. Live like Jesus. Change the World.*

True to our new mission, we volunteered in all kinds of ways to serve our community. One of the most unique was when we agreed to follow the horses in Cochran's annual parade. We ended up "pooper-scooping for Jesus." In hindsight, we should have created some t-shirt designs. We probably could have funded a full remodel of the Children's ministry department with just those T-shirt sales!

Our servant heart for our community grew and grew, until it became commonplace for everyone from event organizers to the City office to call the church asking how many volunteers they could expect from Bow Valley Baptist Church. We loved Cochrane so well that they began to expect it. They sought us out when they had a need. They saw our congregation as one desiring to serve our community.

We crossed the tipping point of our community actually feeling like we were a valuable part of the community. We tried to serve in ways outside and inside the church that showed Jesus' love to our community and served them in ways that made sense to our town and its people (more on that later).

As we loved unconditionally, lives began to transform around us. As Scripture says, They will know we are Christians because we love one another, simply because we had the audacity to love our community like Jesus taught us. We saw much larger numbers of people coming to Christ and being baptized than the church had known in quite some time.

We even started planting *other* churches to reach yet more people in Cochrane.

Today, eight years later, that church continues to love and serve the community of Cochrane. One newer initiative is called The Good Food box, which provides people with healthy fruit and vegetables at a very reduced price and has been a great blessing to the community. The distribution grew so much that the church auditorium had to start being used as the distribution location.

If you lead or serve at a church, if you are involved in church planting or if you desire to be, I implore you to focus on the harvest!

How Bad Is It?

For decades, mainline protestant denominations have been losing members at alarming rates in the US. For instance, between 2000 and 2015, the Presbyterian Church USA, the Episcopal Church, and the United Church of Christ lost 40% of their members.[8]

Did you catch that? A 40% loss in a mere 15 years!

Protestant Evangelical churches and denominations saw a slight increase in church memberships during the first decade of the 21st century,[9] but everything has changed in a post-COVID world.

Reporting of church attendance by denominations and traditions of all stripes show the *lowest* attendance rates ever seen in America's history, *including* conservative evangelical churches.[10]

Did you see that statement? Read it again…

---

8   Jean Hopfensperger, "As Churches Close in Minnesota, A Way of Life Fades," *Minnesota Star Tribune*, July 8, 2018, https://www.startribune.com/as-minnesota-churches-close-a-way-of-life-fades/486037461/.

9   "U.S. Religious Landscape Survey: Religious Beliefs and Practices," Pew Research Center, June 1, 2008, https://www.pewresearch.org/religion/2008/06/01/u-s-religious-landscape-survey-religious-beliefs-and-practices/.

10   "The State of Church Attendance: Trends and Statistics," *churchtrac*, 2025, https://www.churchtrac.com/articles/the-state-of-church-attendance-trends-and-statistics-2023.

Across the US and Canada, we are seeing the lowest attendance rates *ever*—across all denominations.[11] Ever.

Remember the statistics I shared in the introduction: An average of 135 churches close their doors permanently every week in the US. Approximately 4,500 churches close annually, while only 3,000 new congregations are birthed.[12]

The Vice President of Research and Planning for the National Council of Churches estimates that roughly a quarter of all existing US churches will close their doors within the next few years—that's roughly 100,000 congregations permanently shuttered.[13]

"Since the 1990s, large numbers of Americans have left Christianity to join the growing ranks of U. S. adults who describe their religious identity as atheist, agnostic or 'nothing in particular.'"[14] This accelerating trend is reshaping the US religious landscape, leading many people to wonder what the future of religion in America might look like.

---

11   Timothy Keller, "The Decline and Renewal of the American Church: Part 2–The Decline of Evangelicalism," Life in the Gospel, 2022, https://quarterly.gospelinlife.com/the-decline-of-evangelicalism/.

12   Yonat Shimron, "Study: More Churches Closing Than Opening," RNS: Religious News Service, May 26, 2021, https://religionnews.com/2021/05/26/study-more-churches-closing-than-opening/.

13   Rick Reinhard, "Tsunami of Chuch Closings Poses Crisis and Opportunity," Public Square: A CNU Journal, August 13, 2024, https://www.cnu.org/publicsquare/2024/08/13/tsunami-church-closings-poses-crisis-and-opportunity.

14   "Modeling the Future of Religion in America," Pew Research Center, September 13, 2022, https://pewrsr.ch/3qADCA4.

47% of Americans said they belonged to a church, synagogue, or mosque, the first time church attendance has ever dropped below 50% in American history.[15]

According to the Survey Center on American Life, "More than one-third (34 percent) of Generation Z are religiously unaffiliated, a significantly larger proportion than among millennials (29 percent) and Generation X (25 percent)."[16]

"The projections show Christians of all ages shrinking from 64% to between a little more than half (54%) and just above one-third (35%) of all Americans by 2070. Over that same period," those who claim "no religion at all" is expected to "rise from the current 30% to somewhere around 52% of the U.S. population."[17]

What about Canada? Christianity is in sharp decline there, as well. In 2011, 67.3 percent (about 22.1 million people) of Canadians said they were affiliated with a Christian religion. In 2019, that number had dropped to 63. 2 percent. Catholicism, Canada's largest denomination, now accounts for 32 percent of Canadians, down from 46.9 percent in 1996.[18]

---

15   Jeffrey M. Jones, "Church Attendance Has Declined in Most U.S. Religious Groups," Gallup, March 25, 2024, https://news.gallup.com/poll/642548/church-attendance-declined-religious-groups.aspx#:~:text=Nearly%20All%20Faiths%20Seeing%20Declines, over%20the%20past%20two%20decades.

16   "Is Gen Z a Lost Cause for the Church?" *Denisonforum*, December 12, 2023, https://www.denisonforum.org/current-events/is-gen-z-a-lost-cause-for-the-church/#:~:text=According%20to%20the%20Survey%20Center, many%20false%20hopes%20the%20Enemy.

17   "Modeling the Future of Religion in America," Pew Research Center, September 13, 2022, https://pewrsr.ch/3qADCA4.

18   Ashleigh Stewart, "'Gone by 2040': Why Some Religions Are Declining in Canada Faster Than Ever," Global News, January 8, 2022, https://globalnews.ca/news/8471086/religion-decline-canada/.

By 2021, only 53.3% of Canadians identified themselves as a part of the Christian religion in the 2021 census.[19]

Stop and do that math, ehh? A 14% drop in a decade?

This book is not about statistical analysis. The point is, the Christian church (composed of people claiming Christianity) in the United States and Canada is dying, and the rate is accelerating overall.

Even though there is data about this everywhere, as I talk with Church leaders around the US and Canada, one thing I have noticed is *a decided lack of recognition* of this very serious death and decay within organized denominations.

Few seem to recognize the *severity* of the root rot affecting our ability to effectively evangelize the current generations for Jesus and lead *the "prevailing church" that Jesus promised to build* (Matthew 16:18).

On city squares throughout New England (the northeast United States where I currently serve) sit stunningly beautiful churches, planted at the original development of many New England communities, the heart of the Great Awakening.[20] These buildings were once the vibrant central hub of society, integral to daily life among the residents. But now, most are a shell of their former significance within the community, with a handful of weekly attenders, if they are still open at all.

---

19 "Ethnocultural and Religious Diversity–2021 Census Promotional Material," Statistics Canada, November 14, 2022, https://www.statcan.gc.ca/e.n/census/census-engagement/community-supporter/ethnocultural-and-religious-diversity

20 "Great Awakening," History, 2025, https://www.history.com/topics/european-history/great-awakening#section_1.

How can it be that four out of the five New England states are ranked as the "least Christian"[21] in America? What happened to the Great Awakening that New England experienced so dramatically from 1730-1740?

What do you sense the Spirit of God saying to you about what you have just read?

Now let's flip the switch for a minute…

George's Decision

Let me take you to a KFC restaurant in Maritime Canada, a few years ago. I sat across the table from a man named George. His hands were literally trembling as he described a community near the town where he grew up.

Why were his hands trembling as he wrapped them around that "finger lickin'" food? He felt a calling to plant a new church. The town had a known (and well-deserved) reputation for drugs. He struggled with the gravity of transplanting his young family to that area.

When we toured the town together, we passed a number of drug deals, happening right on the main street. Not that everyone in town was part of that culture, but there was certainly a major problem, not only with drugs, but also with such casual acceptance of its existence in the community.

George asked, "Gary, is God calling me here to plant a church and to share the Gospel with these people?" After many

---

21   "Least Religious States," Wisevoter, https://wisevoter.com/state-rankings/least-religious-states/.

conversations and prayers, we both agreed that God was calling him.

And so, George moved his family to this little town and began his daily routine…Exercise, breakfast and a few hours spent in prayer and Bible reading. He would then spend his mornings developing the new church and his afternoons golfing. Just kidding! He would spend his afternoons out sharing the Gospel, visiting every home in town, then through the valley, until he had knocked on every door in town and the surrounding countryside.

George is a gifted evangelist and many, I mean *many*, people came to know Christ through his efforts. The baptisms were a sight to behold and even the community would come out and stand on the bridge over the river to watch those baptized come up out of the cold waters of the beautiful Canadian river, making a public statement to their newfound faith.

This new church was born and hundreds have been born again through this ministry. And the drugs? Today you would never know the community had ever faced a drug problem.

How would you compare your current church activities to George's? Are you seeing hundreds come to faith in Christ? Do you see so many new converts that you have to cause a city-wide spectacle to baptize everyone?

George did what Jesus asked him to do—seek and save those which were lost. He still pastors that church to this day. In fact, he continues to ask me to pray for Gospel conversations he is getting ready to have.

What did the Holy Spirit do in your head and heart as you read this story? Would you describe his story as unique? Does it have to be?

What would have to change in your church, for you to experience this kind of radical transformation in your own community?

These two pictures—the near-empty historic churches of New England versus the fast-growing, faith-planted churches like my buddy, George's—shape the crux of my message throughout the pages of this book.

What we need is a wake-up call. We need to look at the root issues underlying the modern Body of Christ in North America. I need you to find the worst sounding alarm on your cell phone you would never want to use and set it off. Use that blaring noise as a wake-up call in your head, heart, and church.

As church leaders wake up, we need solutions that are both practical and tailored to your local church and community's unique needs. In this book and through my Church Planting Pathway training, I will seek to provide those resources for you.

Way more people are dying every year than the current North American church is leading to Christ.

Can you please re-read that last sentence??

In the last two decades Canada and the United States have seen steep declines in church attendance. Here's what it would take to change that…

First of all, you need to be convinced something radical has got to change. Are you convinced? If not, walk with Jesus in the Gospel of Matthew for a moment…

> [3] Whenever crowds came to Him, He had compassion for them because they were so deeply distraught, malaised, and heart-broken. They seemed to Him like lost sheep without a shepherd. [7] *Jesus understood what an awesome task was before Him*, so He said to His disciples, "The harvest is plentiful but the workers are few. Ask the Lord of the harvest to send more workers into His harvest field." Matthew 9:36-38

Ask Jesus to give you His compassion for the people of North America. Ask Him to help you understand what an awesome task is in front of you. Yes, stop and ask Him right now…You and I…We can walk into the North American harvest together and I am committed to helping you do that in this book!

When we get to part 2, I'll introduce you to the Church Planting Pathway. I believe this tool is the best, most straightforward way to develop your Great Commission assignment into a comprehensive, attainable strategy to see lives transformed by the Gospel of Jesus Christ.

And then, in part 3, we will shift gears a bit and focus on how to implement everything we will have discussed, in your own community. Practical application is my favorite part (behind sharing the good news about Jesus with people who haven't met Him yet)!

But first, I want to talk about *you*—what you need in order to be successful in church planting, in pastoring, in harvesting alongside Jesus, in partnership with the Holy Spirit.

Let's go…

Self-Assessment: Who Cares?

Take a moment to reflect on the wake-up call. Rate yourself on a scale of 1-5 (1 = Strongly Disagree, 5 = Strongly Agree) for each statement. Be honest—this is for your growth, not judgment. Add up your score, then check the scoring key below. Your answers will reveal if you're ready to face the root rot and step into the harvest.

1. I recognize the severity of church decline in my community (e.g., closing churches, low attendance among younger generations).
2. I feel a sense of urgency or grief about the "root rot" in North American churches and its impact on the lost.
3. Stories like George's inspire me to compare my church's activities to his harvest-focused approach.
4. I am willing to make radical changes in my church or planting strategy to prioritize seeking and saving the lost.
5. The Holy Spirit is stirring compassion in me for the "sheep without a shepherd" in my area, motivating me to pray for more workers.

Total Score: _______ / 25

Scoring Key

- **5-10: Asleep at the Wheel** You're in denial about the decay, or the stats and stories haven't hit home yet.

That's okay—God's wake-up call is just starting. Re-read Matthew 9:36-38 and ask, "Lord, would You break my heart for the lost?" Share your score with a trusted friend; their perspective might jolt you. You're not alone, but the harvest needs you awake.

- **11-15: Stirring but Stuck** The root rot's sinking in, but urgency hasn't gripped you. George's story sparked something, but change feels daunting. Good start! Journal: "What would have to change in my church to see hundreds baptized?" Pray the alarm blares louder. Connect with a planter like George.

- **16-20: Awakened and Ready** The decline hits hard, and you're grieving for the lost. You see the contrast between empty New England steeples and George's river baptisms. Momentum's building! Act: List three "radical shifts" for your church (e.g., prioritize evangelism over programs). Share with your team—let's talk; email me your thoughts.

- **21-25: Harvest Heart Ignited** You're convicted, compassionate, and committed—the Spirit's moving! Like George, you're trembling with purpose. Celebrate, then charge: Set a "wake-up alarm" prayer time for the harvest. Mentor one person this week to join you. You're the worker God's sending—let's see transformation.

What stood out most from this chapter? What's one step you'll take today?

Chapter 2

You Are God's Harvester

"The fields are white unto harvest—pray
for more harvesters."
–John 4:35

Here's the thing—people only know what they know. People also have only experienced what they've experienced. "What does that mean, Gary?" you're probably asking yourself. I'm glad you asked.

For the most part, people are living out of their knowledge and their experience. You've probably heard the story of the new bride preparing a roast for her husband. As she dutifully cut off one end of the meat before placing it into the pan and sliding it into the oven, her husband asked her why she removed such a large chunk from the end. She replied that it was how her mother had always cooked a roast. This conversation prompts the bride to ask her mother the reason why she does it that way. Mother's reply? "That's how your grandmother always did it." When the two women ask Grandma why she always cut off the end of the roast, she replies, "Because my pan was so small, that's the only way the roast would fit."

The moral of this story is that we tend to do things merely because we've seen it done that way before, irrespective of the current situation. Even as we love to quote Isaiah 43:19, "Behold, I do a new thing," we don't often consider the *new thing* God wants to do.

One of the wisest men I have ever known always used to say, "People do what makes sense to them." Most of the time, what people know and what they've experienced will dictate the way they go about doing things.

Most church leaders, whether pastors, church planters, or serious Christ-followers who are a part of churches, do what they do because of what they have seen others do. All of us have a certain set of experiences and knowledge. We typically live our lives and make our choices based on that set of experiences and knowledge.

Most pastors and even church planters have never experienced the radical transformation of an entire community like George Storey did. Most have never asked, like Bow Valley Baptist did, "Would anyone in our community miss our church if it were not here?"

As we've discussed, churches in North America are plateauing and dying. Are the people in these churches not sincere? I'm sure they are. Do most of the people in these churches have a heart to know and love Jesus? I believe most of them do. So what's really going on?

The sad reality is that most Christians, even some *pastors*, have never actually led a single person to a personal relationship with Christ. This is the polar opposite of Jesus' assignment, what we call "The Great Commission," where Jesus directs His disciples to "…go and make disciples of all nations, baptizing them in the name of the Father and of the Son and of the Holy Spirit, and teaching them to obey everything I have commanded you" (Matthew 28:19-20).

How many people do you know who have led multiple people to Christ?

Most church leaders, pastors, and denominations are not thinking outside of their current level of knowledge or experience. This is also true for organizations and denominations that are planting churches. Because of this, we are seeing a dying church.

In most cases, it's certainly not about working harder. Most pastors are overworked. Most church planters do not have enough hours in a day. Many Christians are already feeling maxed out with life, family, jobs, serving, and (you fill in the blank).

Let me be clear with you…I'm not getting ready to ask you to pull something off that you are trained to do. I'm not asking you to apply "three simple steps" for a guaranteed turnaround. I'm actually asking you to walk into something **you can't do!**

What? I said, I'm asking you to walk into something **you can't do!**

Welcome to the impossible…Welcome to the real IMF (Impossible Mission Force from the *Mission Impossible* movies). This is God's thing. It's supernatural. It's other-worldly.

This is a new era in Christianity in the North American church. And we need people who are willing to do things they've never done before, in order to see *results* they've never before seen.

Lives literally hang in the balance. Salvation and *eternal life* hang in the balance.

You have lived in the realm of your own experiences, but God wants to push you out of everything you've known before and guide you into a new place. Like Abraham, (Genesis 11-25), you are invited to leave what you have known, the place of your people, your past, to walk down roads you've never walked before.

Or, you can choose to remain where you are and continue to watch the Church die around you.

Are you willing to travel a new path, one much different than the one you would normally choose? (I'd love for you to send me a note to tell me about your decision!)

My heart's cry is for you to experience something you've never experienced before—the joy of working diligently in an abundant harvest field, joyfully serving alongside the Holy Spirit as He transforms hearts and minds into Christ-likeness.

Many people who are following Jesus are doing what they know in the way they know how to do it. What is this accomplishing for us? It's giving us the stats we just read about.

Jesus realized what he was calling us into. Look at how he even described it: "Remember, what is humanly impossible is possible with God" (Luke 18:27).

Or how about this one: "So the impossible is possible with God" (Luke 1:37).

Once again, let me welcome you into the impossible. From the birth announcement of Jesus to a rich man being able to enter into God's kingdom…

We are finding that the impossible becomes possible with God.

Jesus was really straight up about it. He said, "I am the vine, and you are the branches. If you abide in Me and I in you, you will bear great fruit. Without Me, you will accomplish nothing" (John 15:5).

Now, this does not mean you can't do anything. But, rather, the idea is that you can't do anything without Him that will last *beyond* this life.

So, let me ask you again. Are you willing to step into the impossible? Are you done with being part of the 80% of churches that are plateauing or dying? Are you ready to see the new church you plant *actually* reach lost people?

Push the pause button…Stop and answer the questions above. Whether you are a pastor, church planter, or a committed Christ follower in a church, I'm serious…Stop and answer the questions above. I've got the time to wait for you to consider it…(I'm humming the *Jeopardy!* song.)

I will never forget serving as an associate pastor, under a gifted church planter. I was able to experience seeing a large number of people come to Christ. Our church planting leader, Andy, would go door to door, sharing the Gospel and meeting people, throughout a booming part of northwest Omaha. Our church quickly grew to a few hundred people, most of whom had not been Christians prior to meeting Andy.

Through Andy's leadership, I saw the example of someone who was passionate to see people come to Christ. I had actually never seen a person be that passionate about ministering. He would go door-to-door introducing Himself and the idea of the new church and its desire to see people know Jesus personally.

You Need A Vision

You may well be my people if you already feel your heart gripped, captivated by the possibilities that the Holy Spirit is whispering in your ear. He is drawing you, wooing you into uncharted territory.

The downside is that this calling is both new and different, which is undoubtedly scary. The upside is that it's leading you to a deeper connection with Jesus–seeing and experiencing His deep love for people.

Will you join me in this grand adventure? This chasing after the lost sheep (Luke 15:3-7)? Did you know that it could be this way? Will you give the Holy Spirit room to move in your heart and in the lives of your current congregation to transform your community for Jesus? Will you ask Jesus to help you see the "fields that white unto harvest" as He sees it?

This is a holy moment… Stop and pray and use the above questions to drive your prayers deeper into the heart of Jesus.

How could your community be transformed? What would your community look like if you cultivated a mindset like the

Love Cochrane movement, or like my buddy, George, or my church planting pastor, Andy?

Andy was willing to go door-to-door for Jesus. George spent his afternoons meeting people, listening to their hearts, their fears, their real selves, and sharing about a Jesus who loves them. Contrast their people-focused mission mindset with the quiet, staid, systematic church missions that are far more common amongst our denominations. What does change require? Just an unself-centered, unself-focused approach to reprioritize your resources and your time.

One of the most painful things that I hear, pretty regularly actually, is that, "Nobody talks about church planting in New England like you do." Why not? Why aren't more people talking about these things?

I just can't say this enough: More churches close annually than new churches are birthed, by a factor of three to one.[22] That's roughly a net loss of up to 7,000 churches each year!

What are we doing? How can this be?

We're praying for more harvesters, working to plant new churches, and yet America and Canada are getting more and more lost every year.

Many in the church planting world are good, godly men and women who are diligently following a fixed, formulaic process, which worked a decade or two ago, but today we are living in a vastly different culture.

---

22   Carey Nieuwhof, "Why Churches are Closing Faster Than Opening," YouTube, January 8, 2025, https://www.youtube.com/watch?v=7FAP6cuPzcY.

Today's culture requires new methods, new engagement strategies.

I'm not promoting anything outside of what the Bible teaches but rather a shift beyond your current experience, your current systems and methods.

In order for us, collectively, to reach those multiples of salvation I mentioned back in chapter 1, double or triple the number of souls led to Christ, see explosive new numbers of churches planted, and see non-evangelizing churches evangelizing, an earthquake needs to take place in the heart of God's people. It will require an unselfish response. Most churches will have to give up beloved but ineffective programs in order to reprioritize their resources: people's time, treasure, and energy towards evangelism.

A pastor friend has challenged his congregation to see the salvation of 500 new believers over the coming five years. That's 100 salvations a year! Wow!

What kind of shifts would you need to make to see something like this? If you stretch your faith, what vision would you have for evangelism in your church? How many people would you love to see come to Christ in the next five years?

My friend and supervisor with the Christian and Missionary Alliance, District Superintendent Trevor Skalberg, issued a surprising vision and challenge to the fifty churches in his district. He presented a radical dream of doubling the number of churches in the coming decade, so more and more New Englanders can have an opportunity to hear the Gospel. He is shifting the narrative that the American church is hopelessly dying. I was so excited about this vision that I applied for the job of Church Planting Director for Trevor's district, in order to see this vision come to fruition. This vision is inspiring, and God is using it to ignite a great work of God's Spirit throughout New England.

What would it be like if more leaders like Trevor led with this kind of vision? What would your vision look like if you doubled the size of your ministry?

It's in His strength and power that you can walk into the impossible.

When my wife and I were raising our four kids, there was one Scripture I shared with them more than any other: "For I can do *everything* through Christ, who gives me strength" (Philippians 4:13 NLT).

Here's another key verse for our conversation moving forward: *"Here's the knowledge you need*: you will receive power when the Holy Spirit comes on you. And you will be My witnesses, first here in Jerusalem, then beyond to Judea and Samaria, and finally to the farthest places on earth" (Acts 1:8).

Now, I'm glad that we are on the same page, titled "*Impossible,*" together. I am so grateful you are agreeing to step into it. You are actually stepping into a different place, much like what happened to the Israelites here from their story in the book of Joshua.

The leaders were going through the camp of the Israelites giving them their marching orders and they told them this…

> *"Tomorrow,* you will know it is time to go when you see the Levite priests carrying the covenant chest of the Eternal One, your God. Follow the chest so that you will know where you're supposed to go *because you have not been this way before.* But stay about half a mile away from it. Don't come any nearer than that *as you march"* (Joshua 3:3-4; italics added).

Just as the Levite priests were the ones to follow into the great unknown, I believe God has put this book into your hands as a Christian leader in North America, so you can know where to go. But, be ready. To go where you have never gone before and *do* and *act* in such a way that is quite different from your normal, you will have to be courageous and prepared to face many challenges.

Those challenges you can expect to face are what we will discuss in chapter 3. I want you to be prepared to face them head-on, with boldness, believing you can do all things through Christ who gives you strength! (Philippians 4:13).

Self-Assessment: You Are God's Harvester

At the end of this chapter, pause and reflect on your readiness to step into the impossible harvest. Rate yourself on a scale of 1-5 (1 = Strongly Disagree, 5 = Strongly Agree) for each statement. Be honest—this is your wake-up call. Add up your score, then check the scoring key below. Your answers will reveal if you're stuck in the known or ready to follow God into the unknown.

1. I recognize that my current knowledge and experiences are limiting my church's impact on the lost in my community.

2. I am willing to leave my comfort zone and try new methods for reaching people, even if they feel impossible.

3. Stories like George's or Andy's inspire me to prioritize door-to-door evangelism or community service over traditional programs.

4. I feel a divine curiosity about the lost in my area (e.g., unreached groups, dying churches) and am ready to pray and fast over it.

5. I am committed to reprioritizing my church's time, treasure, and energy toward the harvest, even if it means giving up beloved but ineffective programs.

Total Score: _______ / 25

Scoring Key

- **5-10: Stuck in the Known** You're doing what makes sense from your experience, but the harvest is calling louder. That's okay—God's inviting you to the impossible. Re-read Joshua 3:3-4: follow the Ark into uncharted territory. Journal one "new thing" God might ask you to try (Isaiah 43:19). Share your score with a trusted friend; their nudge could be the push you need.

- **11-15: Stirring for Change** The roast story and George's transformation hit home—you see the limits of old ways. Good start! Pray Matthew 9:36-38 for compassion and workers. List three shifts (e.g., door knocking like Andy) to reprioritize for the harvest.

- **16-20: Ready to Step Out** You're gripped by the impossible, like Abraham leaving the familiar (Genesis 12:1). Momentum's building! Fast and pray over one unreached group in your community (Nehemiah 1:4). Rally your team for a "Love [Your Town]" initiative, like Bow Valley Baptist. You're on the edge—take the leap.

- **21-25: Harvest Heart Ablaze** You're all in, trembling like George, ready to knock doors and serve. That's God's fire! Set a vision like Trevor Skalberg's—double your salvations in five years. Start a Top 5 Names prayer list (chapter 10) and a Bible Discovery Group. The impossible's possible with Him (Luke 18:27).

What stirred you most in this chapter? What's one shift you'll make this week? Tell me—I'm here to run with you in the harvest.

Chapter 3

Is It Real or Merely True?

"For many people, the Scriptures are true.
But they're not real."
–Pastor Harold

That statement from my friend and mentor, Pastor Harold, runs through my mind regularly. Is God's Word *real* to me today, or is it merely *true*?

For example… Did Jesus come to seek and save the lost (Luke 19:10)? Does the mind of Christ dwell in me richly (Galatians 2:20)? Does the Spirit empower my witnessing (Acts 1:8)?

Do me a favor. Before you read any further, take this book to a public space, like your favorite coffee shop or park bench. Read it there.

Once you're settled, ask yourself: Am I living an Acts 1:8 life? "But you will receive power when the Holy Spirit comes upon you; and you will be my witnesses in Jerusalem and in all Judea and Samaria, and to the ends of the earth."

Are you living in the promised power of the Holy Spirit? Do you truly believe that God doesn't want anyone to perish but for all to come to a saving knowledge of Jesus Christ (John 3:16)?

Look around the coffee shop or cafe where you're sitting right now. See the people around you. Truly see them. The people you see—are they in darkness and lost? This is how the Bible talks about people without Christ. Do you genuinely believe that God deeply desires for each of them to come into a personal relationship with Him? If so, does your conversation with your waiter or your barista suddenly shift? Are you willing to enter into a deeper type of listening conversation with them, to understand what God may be doing in their life, so that you may have the opportunity to give them a chance to hear about Jesus, perhaps for the first time ever? Would you be the first person ever to pray for or even *care about* their salvation?

Are God's promises real to you, or are they merely true? When you know God's promises are true, you can preach them. You can teach. You can write books and sermons. You can memorize them. But when they are real, every facet of your life is transformed by the realities they bring. I learned this idea about the difference between Scripture being true versus real from one of the wisest men I've ever known, Harold Bullock. Harold made a huge investment in my life and the lives of many. He helped me realize that most Christ followers will say the Scripture is true, but for the most part, it does not really shape the reality of their lives. How about you?

That question must be unequivocally decided, deep within your heart, because walking out the reality of God's promises is so very challenging. And yet, it is the way that Christ's heart is formed in you and your thinking. There are reasons this is tough:

1. Most people have never had anyone model for them what it means to live in the reality of the Scriptures.
2. Most have never had Scripture taught to them this way, including pastors.
3. Most have never even considered the difference between Scriptures being true compared to the idea of Scriptures shaping their reality.

Why is this the experience of most Christ followers?

1. Modeling requires a major shift in how to train someone, and few leaders consider those shifts and how they must reset their lives and ministry to do it.
2. Most teaching on Scripture is knowledge-based rather than transformation-based.
3. Few Christians actually need God enough to *have to* lean on the reality of Scripture. If they did, this would lead to no other choice but to live in the reality of the truth and promises of God's Word. We are very self-reliant and live very little by faith. Rather, we live a life of what we can accomplish, when all along Jesus says, "Apart from me, you can do nothing!" (John 15:5).

Beyond these experiences, three main hurdles make *believing* God's Word more *difficult* than we want it to be. These hurdles aren't just roadblocks—they're furnaces, refining what you believe and who you're becoming. Let's dig deeper into each one, because if you're going to build a church and a life where

God uses you beyond the "norms," you've got to face them head-on.

Hurdle 1: God's Path Isn't Easy

"God leads us through places we don't want to go, to bring us to the place we've always wanted to be," one local pastor's wife says. God will drag you through deserts to shape you, to prepare you to be successful in what He knows is coming.

God is not in the business of coddling you. Moses spent forty years in the wilderness, herding sheep, before he was ready to lead a nation. Joseph was sold by his brothers, jailed on false charges, and forgotten for years, all to save millions from famine. God's path is rarely a straight shot. It's a winding trail through places you'd never choose—rejection, failure, loneliness—to forge you into someone who can carry His mission.

As I worked with my buddy George, he learned how to move from truth to reality, and I want that for you, too. A church planter I work with now, Chuck, is also living in the reality of God's word.

It was a warm spring afternoon as Chuck's team and I were prayer-walking in a northern Vermont community with many addiction challenges. On our walk, we spotted James, a skinny, scraggly kid sitting on the curb. He was probably high and definitely hurting. "Hey, you doing okay? Need some food? Can we pray for you?" I asked. James smirked, "How about a beer?" expecting us to walk away. But I laughed and answered, "Can't do that, but I'll grab you a soda. What kind do you like?"

James blinked, hesitated, then said, "Juice, maybe? Been a while since I had some." His voice was small, like he was bracing for a "no." We didn't miss a beat. "Juice it is. Perfect for a day like this." Then James pointed down the street. "That's my girlfriend coming. Can she get some too?" Amber shuffled up, track marks on her arms, teeth wrecked from meth, but her eyes lit up when I nodded. They dragged me into the store like kids on a treasure hunt.

That $2.50 juice? Best investment we ever made. Our mission wasn't about juice. It was about seeing them, loving them, giving them a taste of kindness they hadn't felt in years. We were able to pray for them and share Jesus' love in a way that lifted them, even for a few moments, into His care. Addiction and despair started crumbling, all because we let the Holy Spirit lead us that day.

Chuck finds all kinds of challenges in that northern Vermont town. Sometimes, the days are brutal. Hours of prayer with no fruit. Weeks of chats on the street with guys who'd barely grunt back. But some days, God puts us in the path of people like James and Amber so we can love them right where they are.

God's leading you somewhere too. Maybe it's to a town that's cold to faith or a neighborhood that's forgotten hope. It's not easy, but it's where transformation happens. Romans 5:3-4 says suffering produces perseverance, then character, then hope. You don't discover hope without first navigating the hard road.

Hurdle 1 Self-Assessment: Facing the Hard Path

Pause and reflect on God's refining path. Rate yourself on a scale of 1-5 (1 = Strongly Disagree, 5 = Strongly Agree) for each statement. Be honest—this is your moment to surrender the deserts. Total your score and check the key below.

1. I recognize that God's path often leads through difficult places (e.g., rejection, delay) to prepare me for His mission.

2. Stories like Moses' wilderness or Chuck's prayer-walking inspire me to embrace trials as transformation tools.

3. I am willing to persevere through suffering, trusting it builds hope for reaching the lost (Romans 5:3-4).

Total Score: _______ / 15

Scoring Key

- **3-6: Avoiding the Desert** You're resisting God's hard path, perhaps fearing the unknown. That's human, but it stalls your mission. Reread Romans 5:3-4 and pray, "Lord, shape me in the wilderness." Journal one "desert" you're facing—how can it prepare you? Share with a trusted friend; their prayer might open your eyes.

- **7-10: Stirring in the Sand** The path's starting to sink in, but you're hesitant to walk it. Good—you see the purpose in trials. Fast for one meal this week, asking God to reveal a "desert" for growth. Like Chuck, take a small step (e.g., prayer walk your street).

- **11-13: Traversing the Trail** You're embracing the hard road, seeing hope in suffering. Momentum's building! Rally a team for a "desert challenge"—pray through a trial together. You're forging character for the harvest—keep going.

- **14-15: Forged in the Fire** You're all in, trusting God's deserts for His mission. That's the heart of a harvester! Mentor one person through their wilderness this week. You're ready—let's multiply this.

What surfaced for you in Hurdle 1? What's one "desert" God's using to shape you? Jot it down—we'll build on it as we face the next hurdle.

Hurdle 2: Your Flesh Fights Back

It's easier to scroll through social media than to talk to a stranger about Jesus. That tug to stay comfortable is strong. The Spirit whispers, *Go talk to that guy on the bench*, but your flesh counters, *Nah, I'm late. He looks sketchy anyway.* Matthew 26:41 nails it: "The spirit is willing, but the flesh is weak." Your flesh loves movie marathons, not awkward conversations. It craves applause, not the silence of slow trust-building. It wants Sunday stats, not unseen seeds planted over juice. As a pastor, church planter, and missionary, I've dealt with many people, including my own family, who believed in the truth of Scripture but didn't live in its reality, at least not much. I've been there too.

I must admit, I'd rather prep a sermon than sit with a stranger who smells like last week's trash. But look at Jesus…He touched lepers, ate with sinners, and stayed up all night praying when exhaustion loomed. His human desires didn't win. His mission did. Your own human desires won't win either if you lean into Galatians 5:16: "Walk by the Spirit, and you won't give into your selfish cravings." It's a daily fight. You'll lose some rounds. But every time you push past comfort, say, to buy a juice instead of walking past, you're training yourself to bow to the Spirit.

Hurdle 2 Self-Assessment: Taming the Flesh

Reflect on the Spirit vs. flesh battle. Rate on a scale of 1-5 (1 = Strongly Disagree, 5 = Strongly Agree). Total your score and see the key below.

1. I recognize my flesh's pull toward comfort (e.g., scrolling over sharing) and how it blocks God's mission.

2. Jesus' example (touching lepers, praying through exhaustion) motivates me to walk by the Spirit daily.

3. I am willing to push past my selfish cravings (Galatians 5:16) to plant seeds, even if it feels awkward.

Total Score: _________ / 15

Scoring Key

- **3-6: Flesh in Control** Comfort's winning, and it's keeping you from the harvest. That's the fight, but God's stronger. Memorize Galatians 5:16 and pray it daily. Identify one "flesh pull" (e.g., Netflix) and replace it with a Spirit step (e.g., call a Top 5 Names person). You're not stuck—start small.

- **7-10: Spirit Stirring** You see the battle, but the flesh still tugs hard. Progress! Journal Jesus' examples from the Gospels—how did He push past human limits? Take one action this week: share your faith with one person, no matter the awkwardness.

- **11-13: Walking by the Spirit** You're fighting back, choosing mission over comfort. Keep going! Train your flesh with a "Spirit habit"—(e.g., pray before scrolling). Mentor someone in this hurdle. You're training for the harvest—stay the course.

- **14-15: Flesh Bowing to Spirit** The Spirit's leading, and your flesh is yielding. That's victory! Lead a group through this hurdle—teach them Galatians 5:16. You're a model for the impossible—let's multiply. What does the Spirit whisper to you in Hurdle #2? What's one comfort you'll push past this week? Write it down, and as we tackle the enemy next, remember, the battle's winnable.

Hurdle 3: The Enemy Hates It

Satan is not subtle."Your enemy, the devil, prowls around like a roaring lion looking for someone to devour" (1 Peter 5:8). He wants to devour your joy, your calling, your community's shot at redemption. He'll hiss lies and half-truths in your ear: *You're wasting your time. They don't want God. You're not enough.* He'll amplify every slammed door, every blank stare, every "no thanks" until you're tempted to quit. He did it to Jesus in the wilderness (Matthew 4:1-11). He tempted Jesus to trade the cross for bread, power, and ease. But Jesus didn't give in. In His strength, you do not need to give in either.

George faced temptation, too. In his lost, drug-infested community, the enemy was whispering, *Give up, Pastor. They're too far gone.* But George stood on Ephesians 6:11, "Put on God's armor, stand firm." The enemy hates when you love the unlovable and see the invisible, because every step you take in faith, being Jesus in the darkness, is a bright light in places where there was no (or very little) light before. The enemy is loud, but he's not stronger than the One who's called you. "Greater is He who is in you than he who is in the world" (1 John 4:4). Believe it. Live in the reality of it.

Hurdle 3 Self-Assessment: Standing Against the Enemy

Examine the enemy's tactics in your life. Rate on a scale of 1-5 (1 = Strongly Disagree, 5 = Strongly Agree). Total your score and check the key.

1. I recognize the enemy's lies (e.g., "You're wasting your time") and how they aim to devour my calling.

2. Jesus' wilderness victory and "the full armor of God"empower me to stand firm against spiritual attacks (Ephesians 6:11).

3. I believe "Greater is He in me," and am ready to love the unlovable, shining light in darkness(1 John 4:4).

Total Score: _________ / 15

Scoring Key

- **3-6: Roar Overwhelms You** The enemy's loud, and you're feeling devoured. That's his tactic, but God's greater. Memorize 1 John 4:4 and declare it daily. Identify one lie he's hissing (e.g., "They're too far gone"), and counter it with Ephesians 6:11. You're not alone—pray with a friend.

- **7-10: Hearing the Lion** You sense the prowling, but the roar's still shaking you. Progress! Re-read Jesus' wilderness (Matthew 4) and pray, "Lord, arm me." Take one stand this week: Pray for an "unlovable" person on your Top 5 list.

- **11-13: Armored and Alert** You're suited up, recognizing the enemy's schemes. Keep vigilant! Lead a prayer time against spiritual attacks—use Ephesians 6:11. You're shining light—push further.

- **14-15: Lion on the Run** The enemy's retreating—you're standing firm in God's power. Victory! Mentor someone through this hurdle; teach 1 John 4:4. You're a light in the darkness—let's multiply. What lie is the enemy hissing at you in Hurdle #3? How will you stand firm this week? Write it down. Now, let's arm ourselves with God's real promises.

Fighting Your Hurdles with Truth

In order for you to victoriously conquer Hurdles 2 and 3 and faithfully persevere through 1, you must know, with great certainty, that God's promises are real, not only for the great men and women of Scripture, but for yourself. Not only for men like George, or Chuck, or my friends at Bow Valley Baptist, but for you too.

What Biblical truths need to move in the direction of shaping your reality? These are some that I've memorized over the years, to encourage and challenge me, when I'm struggling to remember that God's promises are *real*:

People are lost without Christ (Luke 19:10).
Apart from Christ, I can do nothing (John 15:5).
Jesus Christ is my life (Colossians 3:4).
With God, nothing is impossible (Mark 9:23).
Christ lives His life through me (Galatians 2:20).

No one wants to hear the Gospel anymore—or do they? (Acts 1:8).

The devil is real and wants to destroy people (1 Peter 5:8).

There is a true spiritual battle, a wrestling match, taking place in the world today (Ephesians 6:12).

God is creating *opportunity* for me to seize (Colossians 4:5).

The Lord of the harvest is preparing workers to help; my assignment is to call for them (Matthew 9:37-38).

What Scriptures would you add? What ideas above, or others in the Bible, do you struggle with allowing them to shape your reality? Share your ideas with me here.

I come from a broken family. My parents divorced when I was twelve. After the divorce, I was never very close with either of them. When I was thirty-three, with two kids and a third on the way, I told my mom about God's call on our lives to go to Montreal, Quebec, Canada. At that time, only 0.3% of the Quebecois people were followers of Christ. She believed in missionaries and would have agreed they were important. I believe she'd even say Jesus told us to "go into all the world." She'd agree with all of that. But she told me, in no uncertain terms, she'd never come see me in Canada. We chose to go anyway. And she didn't come until many years later, when I brought her into our home to care for her as she battled dementia, not even knowing where she was. She believed in many truths of Scripture, but they weren't real for her.

Here's another example: I told a mom in one of the churches I pastored that I believed her son would one day be a pastor. She emphatically replied that her son would never be a pastor. I asked why. She said they didn't make enough money. I pressed a little, and she wouldn't budge. There are many Biblical truths about money, God's call, and committing our kids to God that could apply here. I'm sure she'd have said she believed at least some of these Scriptures were true, but they wouldn't apply to her if they didn't align with her position about her son. These Scriptures weren't shaping her reality.

Examine Your Own Hurdles

One conversation that I find myself having with nearly every new person I meet, whether they are struggling with their calling to plant a new church or strengthen an existing one, is this: You have no idea how many things that you're doing that are *limiting* what God can do.

My next challenge to them is always: Ask God right now. What are you doing (or neglecting to do) that is *limiting* what He can do right now? What is my church or my organization doing that is limiting what God could do? Many times, most times, you need someone besides yourself who can help you answer these questions. This is why I invite you, at the end of the book, to have a brief conversation with my team. We all need someone to help us see what we cannot.

What about you? Stop and ask God now. What are you doing (or neglecting to do) that is *limiting* what He can do right now?

What did He just say to you? What thoughts are coming to the surface from the depths of your heart? You should also ask someone you trust to look at your life, your church, your organization; ask them to answer that question for you, too.

What lies have you heard so often that you've begun repeating them yourself? What beliefs are holding you back? *It's too hard. No one wants to believe in God.* What perspectives are holding you back? *They don't see things the way I do.*

The only way you'll ever change is if you change your perspective, the way you look at what you see in front of you. What are you valuing that's holding you back? Like my stories of my mom not wanting us to move to Canada, and that parishioner who didn't want her son to become a pastor, these are both quick examples of people who parroted the lies of the enemy.

How would you respond when the people you love the most disagree with what God has asked you to do?

When people disagree with God's calling on our lives, they generally think they are acting out of their love for us. Unfortunately, too often, they've actually allowed the enemy of our souls to speak fear, intimidation, or doubt into their hearts, which they then repeat to us. Ask God to help you examine what you say so that what you say, how you lead, and how you live, release your life and others into His realities.

We Have Seen the Enemy and He Is Real

One major Biblical truth that many Christians describe as true is that there is a God and there is a devil. A 2023 Gallup poll found 86% of people who attend church weekly believe there's a devil—yet other polls show much lower numbers[23]. Even though the Bible is explicit about this truth, a few years back, a whopping four out of ten Christians said they believed Satan is merely a *symbol* of evil, rather than an actual entity. These two disparate statistics go back to the question that I asked you at the beginning of this chapter: Are God's promises, found in the Bible, *real* to you, or are they merely *true*?

What these statistics tell me is that most Christians say they believe the devil is true, but they have never thought the devil is involved in their reality somehow: "The Bible talks about it, but he's not concerned about me," one might say. Yet, that's not what Scripture says. He has disastrous plans for your life, the complete opposite of God's plans for you (1 Peter 5:8).

Here's a reality-shifter for you: I was traveling in Canada with a group of trainers in church planting, including my dear friend Buck, a Cree First Nations man who serves as mayor, pastor, and advocate for his community. Buck and I had built a deep trust—through listening to each other's stories, sharing meals, and walking together in his world and mine. He'd invited me into his community, about six hours north of Winnipeg, Manitoba, because he believed God was calling us to partner in reaching his people with the Gospel, honoring their heritage while pointing to Jesus' love.

Early in the evening, Buck shared with us about an annual ceremony in his community called "tipi shaking." As a

---

23   Frank Newport, "Belief in Five Spiritual Entities Edges Down to New Lows," Gallup, July 20, 2023, https://news.gallup.com/poll/508886/belief-five-spiritual-entities-edges-down-new-lows.aspx.

respected leader, he explained it with care: a rite of passage where the medicine man would gather the children inside a large tipi, its poles anchored deep in the ground. The ceremony aimed to connect them with their ancestors' wisdom, but Buck, who'd come to know Christ years earlier, saw the spiritual danger it posed. He knew the children were precious to God, and he longed for them to encounter the true hope of Jesus instead of traditions that left them bound.

 "Pray with me," he asked us quietly. "I don't want the kids fearing darkness when they can know the Light."

So, we gathered in the van and called out to God, asking that the ceremony's intended spirits wouldn't manifest, and that the tipi wouldn't shake as it usually did. After 30 minutes to an hour of prayer, Buck got a call from community leaders—they were upset. The medicine man couldn't connect with the ancestors, and the tipi remained still. Buck shared honestly, "We were praying, and God answered." They were furious, but in that moment, God's power shone through, not as a confrontation, but as an invitation to something greater. Buck's heart wasn't to tear down his culture but to lift up Jesus, who redeems and restores. That night opened doors for deeper conversations in the community, and Buck's leadership- rooted in love and respect - continues to impact those who knew him even though he is no longer alive.

How does this true story "hit" your truth and your reality? I've had experiences that stretched me, but Buck's faith showed me the power of building bridges first (we'll talk more about that in Chapter 4), listening to a community's heart before speaking. If you want to see the church vibrant and advancing, you must believe the truth and reality that Jesus has authority over spiritual strongholds—and that the enemy of God does *not* want a thriving North American church. And, you must believe that Jesus is building a *prevailing* church.

To be successful in advancing your current church or planting a new one, to reach the lost in your community, here are some statements that you need to believe are not only true but also *real*:

- **Believe the Word is Both Real and True:** You need to believe what God's Word says—not just believe it, but believe it to be true and real. "If God so loves the world…" (John 3:16), He really does love the world. "Any follower of Christ… has been crucified with Christ… He lives through him" (Galatians 2:20). The Word of God is my reality.

- **You Need to Believe People Really Are Lost Without Christ:** I've heard a pastor quote an atheist who said, "If you believe what you say you believe, you'd be talking to me about it." "We're not to be ashamed of the gospel" (Romans 1:16). It takes courage—share the news in a loving and compassionate way. If something is lost, you'll do anything to find it. If someone is lost, you'll do anything to find them!

- **Know That God Has Called You to the Task:** In Montreal, where there was such great animosity to the church historically, it was hard to believe at times that the task *wasn't* impossible. "Did God ask us to do this or not?" my wife and I asked. But we persevered. When God has called you, and you *know* it, you'll keep going.

What would you add to the list?

The enemy's real, and he doesn't want your church to grow, or your community to heal. And, sadly, if you're not in God's Kingdom, you're stumbling in darkness—and the enemy of God would love to keep it that way.

But you've got the Word. Believe it's real. Believe God loves the world (John 3:16). Believe you're crucified with Christ, and He lives through you (Galatians 2:20). Believe people are *lost* without Him—lost enough that you'd do anything to find them.

Moving from truth to reality changes everything.

Chapter 4

The Bridge Principle

"For the Son of Man came to seek and save the lost."
–Luke 19:10

Imagine standing on the edge of a canyon—jagged cliffs dropping into shadow, a river roaring below, too wild to ford, too wide to leap. On your side, you've got safety, truth, the hope of Jesus. On the other? Lost, hurting, and skeptical people staring back across the gap, unreachable. You shout, but the wind swallows your words. You wave, but they turn away. That chasm is real. Sin, fear, and mistrust. Without a way across, those people are stuck, and so are you.

You need a bridge. A bridge doesn't erase the divide; it spans it instead, connecting what's separated, bearing the weight of every step. It's a lifeline, built with intention, anchored in love, sturdy enough to carry souls from despair to redemption. That's your job, in God's strength: to be the bridge, to close the uncrossable distance between a dying world and a living Savior.

Think of the Golden Gate Bridge—massive, iconic, a marvel of steel and cable. It didn't just appear; engineers studied the tides, the winds, the bedrock, then poured years into crafting something that could withstand earthquakes and storms. Your bridge isn't steel. It's flesh and blood, time and tears. But it's no less deliberate. Every plank you lay is a choice to cross the chasm others ignore. I once met a pastor named Sam who planted a church in a rust-belt town gutted by factory closures. The divide was decades of little hope, wondering if God cared. This community was raw and hurting.

Sam knew this town needed something before they would accept his sermons. He started with soup, serving it at the community center, sitting with folks who'd long given up on God. That soup was the first plank, and over months, it stretched into a bridge that carried dozens to faith. The chasm was daunting, but the bridge closed the gap.

Recently, I was talking with a church planter in Vermont. He was frustrated, struggling to attract new members to his little congregation. He asked me about how to enhance their main spring outreach event, an Easter egg hunt. It was well attended every year, with at least 70-100 families and children showing up for fun and prizes. And yet, he said "as best we can tell, in the 5 years or so that we've been doing this event, we've only ever seen one person come to the church service the next day, following the egg hunt."

I asked him to explain more about how they currently invite egg-hunters to become church attenders. He simply replied, "At the egg hunt, we pass out flyers inviting people to church service the following day." They were disheartened by the lack of transition from fun event to meaningful connection and were discussing doing away with the annual hunt, since it wasn't producing the fruit of new church members that they wanted.

My heart broke over the very obvious issue. He was so close to the trees that he couldn't see the forest. I replied, "Okay, but in this area, with as many lost people as live here, you've got to realize that very few of them even know that attending church is a thing they should do. Few will have even *considered* attending an Easter church service. And of those few, many would probably tell you that hell will freeze over or that the church would be struck with lightning if they were to darken the doors. There is a very small number of people in your community who would even think they *should* do that. The people who come to your event have not planned on coming to Easter church service. So when they get your flyer, it's utterly irrelevant to them."

The planter needed to provide a smaller, more attainable next step. A step that would move them closer to Jesus and a step closer to seeing that hell would not freeze over…

Vermont is an outdoorsy state, and most residents are environmentally conscious, so I asked him, "What if you invited everyone to an 'Under the Snow' event?"

"A what?" asked the pastor.

"As spring arrives and the snow melts, there's always an abundance of trash that can be seen once the snow is no longer hiding it. Easter is a perfect time to invite them to a community-wide trash cleanup event, 'Under the Snow,' sponsored by your church. You can do a short prayer or devotion, or offer a blessing before they head out to clean up their community. Then, afterwards, you can invite everyone to a simple celebration of the day's work, with hot dogs, cocoa, and connecting in your church parking lot. Later, you can have another event scheduled, maybe something for families or parents struggling with teens or something else that begins to build relationships at a deeper level with your community."

You have to build each step of the bridge. They don't know they are supposed to cross the bridge. They only know the chasm exists. You have to first build it and then invite them, step by step, across the chasm. All while you act like Christ and share him as opportunity allows.

Notice that none of this has anything to do with watering down the Gospel or conforming the Word of God to fit someone else's ideas. Rather, you've got to first build a bridge of relationship, of connection, with someone before you can expect them to darken the church doors and risk hell freezing over.

The Bridge Principle is simple: Be the bridge they can walk across.

I will never forget when I met my friend Robert Buck, whom I mentioned in chapter 3 with the tipi shaking. I had been invited to a First Nations community about six hours north of Winnipeg, Manitoba. Buck was the community's mayor, a pastor, and a leader with the government, striving to understand indigenous people.

On my way to the community, the Spirit clearly said, "Don't talk while you are there." That was such a strange thing for me to hear. I asked the Lord, "Did the Spirit just say that to me? Is this from you God?" From the best I could tell, it was from Him.

For literally two days, I said as little as possible, just replying to direct questions, and I just tried to listen. We had many periods of silence. Buck finally said, on Day Three, "I will work with you. You are the first white man who ever listened."

That silence built a bridge, and soon, Buck and I were traveling large portions of Canada together in order to see more First Nations people know and understand the Gospel.

Think about Jesus Himself. He had roughly 66 conversations recorded in the Gospels, and no two were the same. The woman at the well? He saw her shame, sidestepped her defenses, and offered living water (John 4:1-26). The blind man? Jesus spat, made mud, and healed him (John 9:1-12). Jesus tuned into the Holy Spirit, met people where they stood, and built bridges they could cross.

When someone asks you what the three Ls are of real estate, what would you say?

The answer? Location, Location, Location

Here are my 3 Ls for how you live the Bridge Principle:

1. **Locate.** Go where people are. Chuck and I didn't wait for James and Amber to stumble into church—we met them at a grimy gas station. Jesus didn't hide in synagogues; He wandered dusty roads, ate with tax collectors, and lingered by wells. Where's your community hurting? The park? The bar? The corner store? The gym? Go there. Ask

Jesus where he would go in your community. When He tells you, respond.

You can't build a bridge from a distance. Too many churches sit like castles, expecting the lost to scale the walls. But Jesus went out—into the streets, the fields, the homes of real people. If you're called to a community or a people-group, you've got to plant yourself in its pulse. That might mean sipping coffee at the diner where the lonely gather, coaching Little League where parents vent, or showing up at the homeless shelter with more than a handout. Location isn't passive—it's you in pursuit. It's saying, "I'm here because you're here," and letting proximity spark possibility.

2. **Listen.** People don't care what you know until they know you care. I didn't speak much with Buck. I listened. Chuck asked questions and heard James' story while he drank his juice. Jesus heard the woman at the well before He spoke the truth. Note to self: ears on, mouth off. Build trust and care deeply.

Listening is the rebar in your bridge. Rebar, short for reinforcing bar or reinforcement bar, is a metal bar that is used to help increase the tensile strength of concrete. As a result, it helps concrete structures withstand tensile, bending, torsion, and shearing loads. In other words, it makes the bridge sturdy enough to carry the weight of heavy loads—heavy conversations, heavy emotions—from one side to the other.

Words can crumble under pressure, but hearing someone—really hearing them—holds up when storms hit. It's not just nodding along; it's catching the tremble in their voice, the ache behind their sarcasm, the hope they've buried. James didn't need a sermon that day. He needed me to ask, "How are you doing?" and stick around for the answer. When you listen, you learn the shape of their chasm, what's kept them from God, and tailor your bridge to fit. Proverbs 18:13 says, "To answer before listening—that is folly and shame." Don't be like that fool. Listen first.

3. **Love.** Galatians 2:20 says, "I no longer live, but Christ lives in me." Let Him guide you. Chuck didn't plan to buy juice that day. The Spirit nudged him. Love isn't a script; it's a sensitivity to what God's doing in the moment.

Love is the cable that keeps your bridge from buckling. It's Christ in you, flexing through every glance, every dollar spent, every hour given. The Spirit knows what they need before you do. Juice for the homeless man, silence rather than speaking, and living water for the Samaritan woman. When you love through Him, it's not about fixing people; it's about showing them they're seen. John 4:12 says, "If we love one another, God lives in us and His love is made complete in us." That's the power that holds the bridge together, God's love, flowing through you, reaching people, precious in God's sight.

Let me tell you about Maria, a single mom I know who turned her apartment into a bridge. She lived in a rough urban neighborhood—drugs, gangs, despair. The cynicism was so thick you could choke on it. She started small (Location), inviting kids to her place for cookies after school. A safe spot in the chaos. She'd Listen, asking about their day, their dreams, their fights, soaking in their stories without judgment. Then she'd Love by praying over them silently as they munched, slipping in a "God's got you" when the Spirit prompted. One kid, Jamal*, kept coming back. Months later, he brought his mom, then his cousins. Maria's living room became a great place to introduce others to Jesus, much like those early disciples, because she bridged the gap—one cookie, one ear, one prayer at a time.

Maria's story is proof that it isn't about what you *say*—it's about how you *listen* and how you *love*. Remember, Buck didn't trust me because of my words. He trusted me because I stayed quiet long enough to hear him. That's the bridge. It's not flashy. It's not a sermon series or a slick flyer. It's you, showing up, seeing people, loving them like Jesus does.

That $2.50 juice wasn't a strategy. It was obedience. It bridged the homeless man from hopelessness to hope, from the curb to a passionate prayer, prompting him from lost to a little bit further along his journey towards being found.

There is one more L…

4. **Lean.** There is a time to speak. "How can they know unless they hear" (Romans 10:14). If you have followed the three previous Ls, you know when to lean in with words, when to lean back in silence, and when to lean on the Holy Spirit for His direction.

So, pause here. What planks do I need to lay to help people cross the chasm between them and Jesus? Maybe it's a barbecue in the park that meets people in the suburbs hiding loneliness behind picket fences, or a basketball league on a city block where faith's a punchline. Whoever's on the other side, they're not your project; they're God's creation. Bridges don't demand crossing. They simply invite it. You're not forcing faith; you're offering a path, plank by plank, built with presence and patience. The Spirit's your architect; you're the laborer. Trust Him to make it strong. Some people need lots of planks, and some are just a plank away…

Remember, "For the Son of Man came to seek and to save the lost," isn't just a verse—it's your mission (Luke 19:10). Jesus came to seek and save the lost. If that's *real* to you, not just *true*, you'll seek people out. You'll build bridges. Not every bridge needs juice, but every bridge needs you—present, listening, loving. The North American church doesn't have to die if we stop waiting for people to come to us and start crossing over to them.

Are you ready to be the bridge?

KEY TAKEAWAYS

- **The Chasm is Real:** Sin, fear, and mistrust separate people from Jesus. Your role is to build bridges that span it, one intentional plank at a time, like the Golden Gate's engineers studied tides to withstand storms.

- **Be the Bridge:** Don't wait for the lost to cross; go to them, showing up as the lifeline that carries souls from despair to redemption, just as Sam's soup in the rust-belt town connected hurting workers to hope.

- **The 3 Ls in Action: Location**—go where people are (parks, bars, stores); **Listen**—hear their stories without judgment

(Proverbs 18:13 warns against answering before listening); **Love**—let Christ in you guide the moment (Galatians 2:20).

- **Jesus' Model:** He had 66 recorded conversations, each unique, offering living water to the woman at the well (John 4: 1-26)) and mud to the blind man (John 9:1-12). He turned to the Spirit, meeting people where they stood.

- **Build Step by Step:** Like the Vermont planter's "Under the Snow" cleanup leading to deeper connections, start small (trash pickup, not a service invite) to close the gap without overwhelming.

- **Lean on the Spirit:** After Location, Listen, Love, lean in to speak when ready (Romans 10:14)—the Holy Spirit dictates the agenda, turning silence (Robert Buck) or juice ($2.50 for James and Amber) into trust.

- **Your Mission:**"For the Son of Man came to seek and save the lost"—is real, not just true (Luke 19:10). Who's on the other side of your chasm? What plank will you lay this week?

Pause and Act: Name one person or group across your chasm. Pray for a 3L opportunity this week—go, listen, love. Share your plank with me at www. thechurchplantingpathway.com. You're the bridge—start crossing.

Chapter 5

Know The End Game

"I have become all things to all people so that by all possible means I might save some."
–1 Corinthians 9:22

Building a church that thrives isn't about what you think it's about. Before we unpack the Church Planting Pathway in chapter 7, we've got to bust some myths that trip up even the best-intentioned pastors, church planters, and serious Christ-followers. My heart burns to see every North American church alive, vibrant, and Acts 1:8 communities where the lost find hope and the broken find healing and transformation isn't a buzzword but a reality. There is an ever-growing witness, fueled by the Spirit's power. But to get there, you've got to know the end game. It's not a packed pew or a polished service—it's deeper, messier, and infinitely more eternal. Let's peel back the layers and see what's really at stake.

Myth 1: The Church Service Is the Goal

Picture this: You meet a young couple who is struggling, searching, and skeptical. You think, "If I can just get them through the doors on Sunday, they'll meet Jesus, join the choir, and tithe like champs." But is that the end game? Another warm body in a pew? A checkmark on your quarterly report? Pastors feel this tug-of-war: "Go make disciples" (Matthew 28:19), vs. "Show me the numbers attending." It's a tension that gnaws at you. Discipleship is the call, but your leadership is asking for that annual report once again.

Don't get me wrong, church attendance matters. I've poured my life into planting and pastoring churches across the US and Canada. The Bride of Christ is worth fighting for. But the service isn't the starting line and the end game isn't attendance. It's about fulfilling what Jesus commanded.

Take my friend Tom, a pastor in rural Alberta. He spent years chasing Sunday numbers by tweaking worship, begging for volunteers, and guilting folks into showing up. Attendance spiked, then flatlined. So he shifted. He started hosting bonfires in his backyard where neighbors could eat, talk, and be. No sermons, no pressure. One guy, Mike, came for the hot dogs, stayed for the chats, and months later asked, "What's this Jesus thing?" Mike's a disciple now, not because of a pew, but because Tom saw the real goal: life change, not headcounts. Church services *amplify* discipleship. They rarely create it.

Yet, church planters invariably tend to think in terms of church services, rather than finding unbelievers where they are.

I recently participated in a small church plant's kickoff event in a rented hotel conference room. This service had been much-anticipated. The plant team had been praying for a huge turnout. I had traveled from several states away to speak at this inaugural event, yet only five people filled the room that Sunday morning, including the Pastor and his wife. Everyone was embarrassed at the small turnout.

The planter apologized for wasting my time for such a pitiful kickoff. He even suggested we cancel. But I knew God had a powerful message for them. I said, "Let me preach. I'll preach as if there are 200 people there, let's just do it." I spoke on one of my favorite passages," I have come to seek and save that which was lost" (Luke 19:10).

You see, I had already been working with this group, trying to get them to follow the proven steps of the Church Planting Pathway. But the pastor was so focused on the "service." He thought he already knew what his community needed. When I finished my message, the pastor agreed that it was time for his team to focus on evangelizing. They were out in the streets, meeting new people the very next week.

Church services are a natural outgrowth of praying together, worshiping together. But it's not the be-all and end-all. Services aren't the point. The end game isn't attendance; it's *discipleship*. People gathering, connecting, and trusting, then stepping into fellowship when they're ready. The service is a tool, not the point.

Myth 1 Self-Assessment: Beyond the Service

Reflect on whether your focus is on attendance or discipleship. Rate on a scale of 1-5 (1 = Strongly Disagree, 5 = Strongly Agree). Total your score and check the key below.

1. I recognize that chasing Sunday attendance often distracts from the true end game of making disciples.

2. Stories like Tom's bonfires inspire me to create relational opportunities outside church services for life change.

3. I am willing to shift my priorities from "filling seats" to building trust and connections with the lost.

Total Score: _______ / 15

Scoring Key

- **3-6: Service-Centric** Attendance is your main metric, and it's keeping you from the harvest. That's common, but God's call is deeper. Re-read Matthew 28:19 and pray, "Lord, shift my focus to disciples." List three "bonfire-style" opportunities (e.g., backyard chats) for your community. Start one this week.

- **7-10: Stirring for Depth** You see the tug-of-war, but services still pull harder. Progress! Journal: "What if my church closed tomorrow—who would miss us?" Like Tom, host one non-service event (e.g., coffee meetup).

- **11-13: Discipleship Dawning** You're leaning toward life change, seeing services as tools. Keep going! Rally your team for a "trust-building" initiative (e.g., community cleanup). You're aligning with the end game—multiply it.

- **14-15: Harvest-Hearted** Discipleship's your north star—you're ready for transformation. Lead! Mentor one person through a relational step (e.g., invite a skeptic to a meal). You're living the call, so let's scale it.

What does this myth reveal about your end game? What one shift will you make this week? Note it down—as we bust the next myth, remember, the true goal is hearts changed.

Myth 2: "I'm Called Here—That's Enough"

You feel God nudge you to a new place—say, Montreal, Quebec, Canada—and you charge in, Bible blazing, ready to plant a seeker-driven church with a discipling base system that draws on baseball as its model because it worked back in Nebraska. Except… the people struggle to understand it. Why? You didn't get the culture.

There's a reason the Montreal Expos (professional baseball team) didn't make it there. Montreal's got a rich heritage of food, culture, habits, hockey, and wounds from religious institutions. The Apostle Paul said it well, "Become all things to all people…" (1 Corinthians 9:22). So dive into their world. Learn their history. Feel the heartbeat. Connect in ways that make sense.

I tried planting a slick church model in Montreal more than once. However, people there didn't want programs—they wanted authenticity. So I ditched the playbook and started learning more about the people and culture. This led to guys like Luc, a tattooed non-practicing Catholic (which pretty well sums up most Montrealers), who scoffed at my first invite to church. "That's where the bitterness comes from," he said, nodding to a past of religious hurt. But over months of chats over coffee and listening, he softened. He's a believer now, not because I forced a model, but because I learned his language, literal and cultural.

Consider Lisa and Brent, who planted a church in a gentrified Seattle neighborhood. They assumed their hipster vibes would win them points with the community. Nope. The locals saw through the sheen; they craved real. So they pivoted, joined a community garden, dug in the dirt, and asked about their lives. Brent and Lisa didn't preach; they planted. A year later, the new "church" was a dozen folks meeting in a greenhouse, dirt under their nails, and Jesus in their talks.

Location without culture is a bridge to nowhere. Know your soil. You have to give yourself permission for your new church, or even your current church, to be as unique as your community. Remove *your* constraints around what or how the Lord is allowed to move. Give Him permission to do the "new thing" that He desires in this place that He is calling you towards.

Myth 2 Self-Assessment: Embracing the Culture

Examine your cultural fit. Rate on a scale of 1-5 (1 = Strongly Disagree, 5 = Strongly Agree). Total your score and see the key.

1. I recognize that imposing my previous church model on a new community often leads to disconnection.
2. Stories like Luc's or Lisa and Brent's inspire me to learn and adapt to my community's history and heartbeat.
3. I am willing to dive into my soil—studying culture, wounds, and needs—to build a bridge that resonates.

Total Score: _______ / 15

Scoring Key

- **3-6: Model in Charge** Your past model's leading, and it's blocking connection. That's okay—God's inviting adaptation. Re-read 1Corinthians 9:22 and pray, "Lord, show me my community's language." List three cultural elements (e.g., hockey in Montreal) to incorporate. Start observing this week.

- **7-10: Soil Stirring** You see the need to adapt, but the shift feels uncomfortable. Progress! Journal: "What's my community's 'hockey'?" Like Lisa and Brent, try one garden-style step (e.g., join a local event).

- **11-13: Bridge-Building** You're diving into the soil, ready to resonate. Keep digging! Rally your team for a "culture walk"—explore your town's history together. You're aligning—push further.

- **14-15: Harvest-Resonant** You're all in, speaking your community's language. That's the end game! Lead a relational initiative (e.g., community cleanup). You're bridging gaps—let's multiply.

What cultural "hockey" is God highlighting for you? What's one adaptation you'll make this week? Jot it down—as we confront the hero myth next, remember, dependence on Him is the true strength.

Myth 3: It's About You Being the Hero

Here's a sneaky one: You think the end game's on your shoulders. You think, "If I preach better, pray harder, hustle more, the church will thrive." Wrong. You're not the Savior, Jesus is. Too many planters and pastors burn out wearing the hero cape, forgetting John 15:5: "Apart from me you can do nothing." It isn't about your preaching brilliance. But rather it's your dependence on Christ.

I knew a guy, Mark, who launched a church in Detroit with charisma and a killer vision. He was the star…sermons, outreach, and everything else…all him. He was the shining star in the church planting assessment that year. Six months in, he seemed to be doing great, his congregation was growing, but he was dying. Exhausted, on the verge of burnout. He confessed to me, "I thought they needed a show." Then he surrendered, prayed more than he planned, let others lead, and trusted the Spirit. The church didn't collapse; it deepened. People like Seth, a former dealer, found faith not through Mark's shine but through the unassuming, quiet guy that Mark empowered to share his own story, instead of Mark's.

The end game is God's, not yours. You're a conduit, not the current.

Myth 3 Self-Assessment: Releasing the Hero Cape

Examine your dependence on Jesus. Rate on a scale of 1-5 (1 = Strongly Disagree, 5 = Strongly Agree). Total your score and check the key.

1. I recognize that relying on my efforts alone (e.g., charisma, hustle) leads to burnout and misses God's end game.

2. Mark's story inspires me to surrender control, letting the Spirit lead through others, not just me.

3. I am willing to trust John 15:5 ("Apart from me you can do nothing") and empower my team to share their stories.

Total Score: _______ / 15

Scoring Key

- **3-6: Hero Mode Engaged** You're carrying the load, and it's wearing you down. That's the trap, but God's offering rest. Re-read John 15:5 and pray, "Lord, I surrender the cape." Identify one task to delegate this week. You're not alone—start small.

- **7-10: Surrender Stirring** You see the burnout risk, but releasing control feels scary. Progress! Journal: "What's one thing I can hand off?" Like Mark, pray for the Spirit to lead through your team.

- **11-13: Conduit Awakening** You're trusting Jesus more, empowering others. Keep yielding! Mentor one person to share their story. You're flowing in God's current—multiply it.

- **14-15: Fully Surrendered** The Spirit's leading—you're the conduit, not the hero. Victory! Lead a team huddle: "How can we share together?" You're living the end game—let's scale.

What hero cape are you ready to release? What's one delegation you'll make this week? Note it down and remember, dependence on Him is the true power.

The Catch: Making New Disciples Is Messy

Making disciples, the true end game, isn't clean or countable. It's not a packed sanctuary or a viral sermon clip. Sometimes it's slow. Other times, it's shockingly fast. It's relational, unpredictable, and rooted in opportunity. It's buying a guy some juice, staying silent, stoking a fire, weeding a garden, stepping back. It's being "All things to all people" (1 Corinthians 9:22): flexible, Spirit-led, and sacrificial. The catch is that you can't shortcut it. Numbers might impress your overseer, but transformed lives impress God.

Think about it: Jesus' disciples weren't a tidy dozen. Peter denied Him. Thomas doubted. Judas betrayed. Yet Jesus poured into them. He ate with them, walked with them, and died for them. Discipleship took investment, not a service. Your community's no different. That barista you see nearly every day? She might not pray a salvation prayer tomorrow. But every "How's your day?" plants a seed. Every "I see you," waters it. The catch is God's timing is time you don't control and results you don't dictate. It's faith that God's growing what you're sowing. Sometimes quickly, sometimes not.

My challenge to you is to know your end game. It's not a service; it's a movement. It's not a headcount; it's hearts changed. Ask yourself: "Am I seeking the lost, or just filling seats?"

KEY TAKEAWAYS:

1. **Shift Your Metric.** Stop focusing so much on attendance and start counting conversations, connections, moments of trust, and new disciples made. Live out the Three Ls: write down three people you'll invest in this week, not to drag to church, but to love where they are.

2. **Study Your Soil.** Spend a day walking your community—no agenda, just eyes open. Walk and pray about what you notice. What's its history? Its pain? Its pulse? What is God speaking to you about this place? Let that shape how you show up.

3. **Surrender the Cape.** Pray this daily: "Lord, it's Yours, not mine." Release the pressure to perform; ask the Spirit to lead. Then watch Him work through others—your people, not just you.

The North American church doesn't have to die if we chase disciples over reports to the home office. It's hard, slow, glorious, and surprisingly inconvenient. Are you in?

So here we stand. At the edge of what could be, with the North American church's fate hanging in the balance. Part 1 has been about shattering illusions: the hurdles that test us, the bridges that connect us, and true definitions of success. We've seen that it's not about filling seats or forcing formulas. It's about living the Scriptures as *real*, not just true, and pursuing new disciples over reports. But knowing the *why* is only the start. In part 2, we'll roll up our sleeves and dig into the *how*—the Church Planting Pathway, a practical roadmap to grow your community into a living, breathing reflection of Christ's heart.

Ready to build? Let's dive into the Church Planting Pathway in part 2.

PART 2

The Church Planting Pathway

Even Jesus Built Out a Team

"Follow me, and I will make you fishers of men."
–Matthew 4:19

Let's stand on the shores of the ancient Galilee for a moment. The water glints under the sun and nets lie tangled at your feet. Jesus approaches, His gaze unwavering. "Follow me," He says, "and I will make you fishers of men." Your heart pounds— hope stirring, but also uncertainty. You're not alone, in that moment, in that feeling of excitement and trepidation. Peter and Andrew felt it too, ordinary fishermen chosen as some of the first members of Jesus' team. He didn't begin with crowds or a master plan; He started with a handful of misfits, teaching them to reach souls by first reaching theirs.

If Jesus needed a team to launch His mission, why would you attempt to plant a church without one?

This is the most foundational step in order to successfully implement the Church Planting Pathway: Build a *harvest team*. Not a conventional launch team of seasoned believers ready to organize events, but a committed, interconnected group—

often new Christians, raw and real—drawn from the very harvest you're called to reach. The North American church is faltering, not for lack of programs, but for lack of souls saved, disciples made, and communities united in Christ's love. That revival begins with a team, and it starts with you, Jesus, and a small band of brothers and sisters in Christ, ready to reach the harvest.

The Myth: You Need a Flawless Team

Let's confront a misconception head-on: you don't need an elite team of ministry professionals to plant a thriving church. Many planters envision a perfect roster—pastors with advanced degrees, worship leaders with viral YouTube covers, accountants to balance the books. That was not Jesus' way, and it's not ours. Over the past two decades, evangelism and baptisms have declined sharply—studies from Lifeway Research and Barna Group confirm a drop of over 20% in reported baptisms among Southern Baptists from 1999 to 2019 and a similar trend in evangelical engagement.[24] C. Peter Wagner, a professor at Fuller Theological Seminary, once declared church planting "the single most effective evangelistic methodology under heaven."[25]

And yet… what do most church planting organizations, books, and strategies do? They focus on an organized, structured

---

24   "Lifeway Research, "Baptisms Rebound, but Negative Trend Continues in Southern Baptist Churches," January 23, 2024, https://research.lifeway.com/2024/01/23/baptisms-rebound-but-negative-trend-continues-in-southern-baptist-churches/; Barna Group, "Signs of Decline & Hope Among Key Metrics of Faith," March 4, 2020, https://www.barna.com/research/changing-state-of-the-church/.

25   C. Peter Wagner, Church Planting for a Greater Harvest: A Comprehensive Guide (Ventura, CA: Regal Books, 1990), 11.

approach, professionalizing the process with rigid assessments and corporate strategies that prioritize numbers over transformed lives. The actual act of harvesting, the inviting of lost souls into the Kingdom of God, is being neglected.

Consider the 2025 Super Bowl between the Kansas City Chiefs and the Philadelphia Eagles, what I call the "Un-Super Bowl." One team arrived prepared; the other was utterly outmatched. Why? The losing side didn't understand the field. To reach the harvest, you need a team that understands, that *knows,* the harvest—people who share your community's struggles, speak its language, and feel its doubts. Not the spiritually polished, but the newly redeemed, like Matthew, a tax collector shunned by his fellow Jews, or Philip, an unremarkable man by the Galilean waters. Jesus chose unlikely candidates to fish for souls.

Your team must rise from the same soil: authentic, local, passionately committed to seeing lives transformed in the very community you've been sent to reach.

The Reality: Your Harvest Team

The foundation is this: Your first team is not for launching church services—it's a *harvest team,* and it begins with just you and Jesus. Just the two of you, walking together as He shapes you into a fisher of men. Matthew 4:19 is a divine commitment: *"Follow me, and I will make you fishers of men."*

You don't need to gather a ready-made group of Christians from other congregations. In regions like New England—or even across much of North America—such groups are already scarce. That's a blessing in disguise. Too often, long-time believers struggle to connect with the unsaved or the lost. I've seen them, with the best intentions, push away people like Matthew at his tax booth or the woman at the well, their words sounding foreign to those outside our faith.

Why? It's certainly not intentional, but nevertheless, the longer we are Christians, the farther away we move from those old lifestyles, behaviors, and thought patterns. We're becoming more Christ-like, yes, but we're also becoming more Christian-ized. While that's definitely not a bad thing, it does make it more difficult for many of us to remember how we thought, where we hung out, and what we liked to do in our free time, making it more difficult for us to relate.

Your harvest team is different, built from the harvest itself—locals, often new converts, those who know the pain of *being* a lost soul, because they've lived it. Recently.

Jesus modeled this. He didn't start with a mass rally. He found Andrew and Peter, two men lingering by the docks; then He called James and John (Matthew 4:18-22). They then crossed paths with Phillip and Nathanael (John 1:43-51).

It was deliberate, Spirit-led, one heart at a time. You will build similarly, and "Make the most of every opportunity" (Colossians 4:5). God is already at work in your community, preparing people—teachers, mechanics, single parents—who may not want to enter a church but yet hunger for truth. The Holy Spirit is drawing them to you. They are your harvest team.

Why Harvest Teams Succeed

Let me introduce you to Mike, a man who stepped into Pastor Ed's church in Bennington, Vermont. Mike wasn't polished. He had no theology training. He was just a local guy with a rough past, newly gripped by an excited, passionate faith.

Mike had friends who'd never consider church. So Pastor Ed didn't assign him tasks; he simply invited Mike to share his story and bring those friends along. Mike became a bridge of trust, as we discussed in chapter 4. His friends listened to *him*, not a stranger at a pulpit, and through him, salvations began to multiply. Why? Mike understood the harvest—its fears, its skepticism. He could tell Ed, "That analogy won't connect… try this instead." A harvest team that is closely connected to the harvest before them brings credibility and closeness to the pre-Christians that you, as a planter/pastor, are still getting to know.

Contrast that perspective with planters who recruit "experts" from elsewhere. It's like fielding a team for the Super Bowl that's never played the game. They falter—not for lack of skill, or even for lack of knowledge, necessarily, but rather for lack of connection, lack of relatability. New believers bridge that gap. They know why "church" feels hollow to their friends. They can speak the Gospel in ways that resonate. A harvest team brings credibility and connection, speaking the Gospel in ways that resonate, like a local dialect to a weary soul. They're your guide to reaching those far from faith.

Remember my story back in chapter 5, when I was trying to connect to a Montreal community using a baseball metaphor?

I kept striking out until I switched it up and framed my conversations using the more appropriate hockey metaphor instead. Once I changed my language to something that resonated with the local culture, I started making sense.

Just as connecting with a community demands language that echoes its heart, planting a church requires a team that shares its burdens. You cannot reach the harvest alone, nor should you try. The lesson from Montreal applies here: Success hinges on alignment with the people you serve and the partners you enlist. A solitary planter, no matter how gifted, risks missing the mark, just as a misplaced metaphor does not connect to your audience.

The Danger of Going Solo

If you attempt to plant a church alone, you'll exhaust yourself before the first seed takes root. I've watched gifted planters try to be everything, all at once—preacher, counselor, administrator, visionary. They collapse under the weight, their calling diminished. No one can carry the weight of the entire harvest single-handedly. You're not supposed to.

Even Jesus didn't. He could have transformed the world with a single word, but He chose twelve imperfect disciples to share the mission instead. Why? Because God's Kingdom thrives on shared burdens, not lone heroes. Your community needs a pastor, a listener, and a friend—not a solitary figure stretched thin. A harvest team extends your reach and opens doors to relationships you would probably never encounter on your own.

Yet, even with a team, a greater challenge threatens to derail your mission: The weight of institutional systems that prioritize control over calling. While a harvest team amplifies your reach, human-made structures often constrict it, replacing the Spirit's freedom with rigid expectations. The same God who entrusted His mission to a diverse band of disciples calls you to prayerfully consider any such constraints keeping you and your team from the harvest.

Building Your Team with Jesus

So, how do you begin? With you and Jesus, rooted in the 3 Ls from chapter 4—Locate, Listen, Love. Location matters—Cleveland isn't Charlotte. Saskatoon is not Montreal. Once you understand the unique challenges of your city, go where the lost souls are. Go to the markets, coffee shops, and bus stops. Listen to their stories—their losses, hopes, and questions. Love them as the Spirit leads, like Chuck did, buying juice for James and Amber. Then watch who God brings your way. Perhaps a Mike, unrefined but earnest. Perhaps a Maria, whose cookies softened hearts. They're not experts, they're just unique people using their unique gifts and personalities to serve and follow Jesus.

Then, proceed deliberately, as Jesus did. He didn't hurry His disciples; He guided them, sometimes smiling at their missteps and sometimes rebuking (think Peter's fiery outbursts, James and John arguing over who was the "greatest" among the disciples), and remember, He sent them out sooner than expected (Luke 10). You must give people opportunities to serve. For example, not every planter or pastor excels at evangelism. Paul urged Timothy to "do the work of an evangelist" regardless (2 Timothy 4:5). Find those with that gift, equip them with the 3 Ls from chapter 4, and release them to their own assignments.

Recently, at a wedding, I met two young men with kingdom-advancing potential. I asked, "Have you considered planting a church?" They were stunned. No one had asked them that question before. Days later, one found himself praying with a woman over her medical debts and broken family, because he was primed to *see* her, to notice her need for connection to the Father, in the midst of his busy life. Your role is to fish for such leaders, trusting God's provision.

As you work, avoid prescribing a certain church style or format. Your task isn't to impose *your* church model, but to discern Jesus' vision for *His* church (Matthew 16:18). What type of church will best serve your community? A neighborhood gathering? A large launch?

The Church Planting Pathway advises you to spend time in prayer retreats, hearing from Jesus, the Builder of the church, about the type of church He wants you to join Him in building. Some planters dream big then adjust as they begin to grasp the true cost. Others envision grand community service projects, like a maternity home for pregnant women in crisis, but start small, renting a space, rather than waiting until they have raised millions. Hold your vision loosely with open hands, refined through prayer and honest counsel.

If you inherit a launch team of believers, that's valuable, but reorient them to love the lost, lest they demand a church of old hymns, lest they demand a church of old hymns, Vacation Bible School (which sounds like indoctrination school), or anything that needs tons of explanation to someone not yet following Jesus.

Your Challenge: Focus on the Harvest

The North American church need not perish, but it will continue to fade if we recruit teams from the pews rather than the harvest. You're not alone. Jesus is your first partner, and He's preparing others to support you. This week, pray, "Lord, it's You and me—show me one person." Visit a diner, a park, or a corner store. Practice the 3 Ls. Trust God to act, as He has in New England, where one church plant grew to thirty new churches—urban and rural, in languages from French to Spanish—because teams embraced the harvest. Chapter 7 will reveal the full Pathway to shape that team. For now, ask God to bring you your first harvest team member (again, it may be the first person you have led to Jesus) to join you. The harvest awaits, and the Lord is already preparing their hearts for your arrival.

Before we dive fully into understanding the Pathway, there's one more thing I want to discuss with you.

Team Oversight

What kind of "team" or organization or denomination are you teaming up with, or are planning to team up with? We know we need a supporting group (whether that be a network, organization, or denomination) to help us maintain accountability and to provide advice, equipping, and support.

But, I would counsel you closely here…

Most organizations are working from an angle of "you serve the organization," but truly, Jesus' way is that the *organization* is supposed to serve *you*. The difference is a top-down approach versus a bottom-up, field-based approach. A field-based approach allows for flexibility and rapid response to the true, felt needs of you, the planter, and the church you are planting and serving.

Let me share some insights and shifts that organizations, networks, and denominations desperately need to make in order to be a part of turning the tide of the dying church.

Shifts Needed to Reimagine Church Planting Systems

Traditional systems—assessments, funding, coaching, and models—often hinder the very movements they aim to support. I've seen their limitations firsthand, and we've devised a better way through the Church Planting Pathway, which you'll explore in chapter 8. But first, let's delve into the ways in which you'll need to rethink church planting, in order to understand and embrace the new methods of the Church Planting Pathway.

Here's how we rethink these systems to unleash kingdom advance through church planting.

SHIFT 1—Traditional Church Planting Assessments Stifle Movement

A traditional assessment model gathers professionals to evaluate planters over 2-3 days, judging them based on a predefined list of 9-12 characteristics of "successful" planters.

Assessment centers are designed with at least two goals in mind:

Weed out those who are deemed not to have enough of these characteristics to be successful

The stewarding of resources given to church planters to those who will potentially and likely be successful.

This thought process sounds logical. But traditional assessments slow movements. With dying churches outpacing new churches, assessments require large teams of people and can only manage a certain number of planters based on the assessment team. And, typically, they can only be managed once or twice a year.

This limits any form of multiplication and barely allows for *addition (which is not really addition due to the number of dying churches)*.

Another challenge is that they fail to reach new Americans and New Canadian believers, whose diverse gifts and cultural differences don't necessarily fit rigid, traditional assessment criteria. They can also be costly and hard to scale. In the Church Planting Pathway, *the journey itself* becomes the assessment. We equip and counsel planters as they walk with Jesus, and share the Gospel, which allows us to release many more leaders into the harvest

SHIFT 2—Faithfulness-Based Resourcing

Traditional funding gives planters modest support on a three-year timeline, expecting new churches to grow their own income, usually through tithes and offerings, toward self-sufficiency. But, as we've discussed, this can often lull leaders into a false sense of security and cause more harm than help when the financial support inevitably wanes.

We flip this with Faithfulness-Based Resourcing. Funding grows as planters progress through the Pathway's steps, with four increases tied to faithfulness in outreach, disciple-making, team-building, and multiplication. Timelines are flexible; we hold conversations, not cutoff dates for funding. We match the funds planters raise, scaling support as their fledgling congregation grows. This stewards resources while fueling evangelism. It also increases support to the plant as it continues to grow.

SHIFT 3—Advice, Not Coaching

Every church planting book insists on coaches, but are there enough? With such a huge need for new churches, we lack the coaches to match. We offer advice and counsel instead— biblical wisdom from leaders, more abundant and accessible. This equips planters without the bottleneck of narrowly specialized coaching.

SHIFT 4—Harvest-Centric, Not Model-Centric

Assessments often favor "launch" model planters, prioritizing services over new disciple-making. Instead, we counsel church leaders to focus on the harvest. In New England, we support all types of churches in order to reach all types of people in all types of places. Don't take me wrong, I love church services, but what if we poured more energy into harvesting? We should cry out to God to give us fruit that lasts (I discuss this more later in the book) (John 15:16). Let's be harvest centric, not model centric.

SHIFT 5—Movement-Oriented Equipping

We train with free, principle-based materials in multiple languages, designed to raise trainers who multiply training. This equips planters to spark movements, not just manage programs, scaling the Gospel's reach.

SHIFT 6—Finding Planters

Where are the church-planting pastors and pastoral leaders? I've heard this question hundreds of times. The Lord of the harvest says workers are few, but He invites us to pray for more to arrive (Matthew 9:38). For over twenty years, as I've prayed, the Lord of the harvest has led me to planters. And the great news is that The Church Planting Pathway allows anyone with a pastor's heart, character, and doctrinal alignment with our organization to begin with us. In New England, less than two years into utilizing the Pathway, we've seen nearly thirty planters join or prepare to partner with us with more plants, with leaders preparing to start within the next year and even into the next year.

This was done with just fifty churches in our network (district of churches) when we started this. By God's grace, we are on our way to doubling the number of churches we will have in our group in New England in just a few years. What would happen if this happened with the group that you serve? A doubling in ten years or less? (Would you write to me and tell me about what that would be like with your group? I'd love to pray with you that this would happen.)

Many, if not most, denominations, church planting networks, and organizational systems are stifling church planting movement.

Organizations, despite good intentions, often design systems for their own convenience, rather than Christ's mission. For example, assessments that penalize a planter for preaching in a second language. Criteria that value eloquence over zeal. I know a man, a third-language English speaker, who poured his heart into a sermon, only to be told it fell short by a committee of church administrators, more focused on his eloquence than his anointing, his calling.

Years ago, I faced a heart-wrenching moment in Southern Alberta. I had forty church planters ready to serve, their hearts ablaze for the harvest. But the organization I was serving with, at the time, offered only six spots for assessments that year. "They'll have to wait," the leadership said. *Wait?* I was sick to my stomach. In a province teeming with people far from Jesus, I was walking with the Lord of the harvest, finding potential planters eager to start new churches. Yet, the system said no. That day, I knew something had to change, and that I wouldn't stay with that organization much longer.

These systems, born to steward resources, have hardened into barriers, keeping planters from the harvest. Let's not forget: What did Jesus model for us? What can we see in His selection of leaders? What does the OT remind us of how we are supposed to seek out leaders (1 Samuel 16:7)? Remember, David was the youngest, the overlooked one. The traditional models of finding and selecting leaders seem quite different from Jesus' way and even the Bible's way.

The consequences of the broken system are stark. Evangelism and baptisms have plummeted over two decades; the data from Lifeway and the Barna Group confirm the decline. New church planting has slowed, even as existing churches close faster than ever. It's disheartening to follow an organization's rigid steps, believing you're succeeding, only to find that few lives have actually changed, and few new people have been welcomed into the Kingdom of God. Planters share the pain of checking boxes for leaders while the harvest languishes. Systems can be Spirit-driven, but it's rare.

This is a clarion call for planters, pastors, and organizations alike. We need teams rooted in the field, in the community's culture—whether that's Boston, Boise, or Brampton. Not top-down blueprints from a denominational office.

In the 1950s, Chrysler had a unique vision: a car with a record player. An audacious idea, though it failed (special records had to be created, which were overpriced and impractical). It was a daring idea, revolutionary for its time, and ahead of the curve of customer desires. Yet, recall what progressed in the automotive industry: First, cars came equipped with 8-track players, then cassette tapes, then CDs, and now we have an overwhelming availability to stream music to ourselves anywhere, at any time, whether through our cars or our phones. Even though an in-car record player didn't quite pan out, its novelty paved the way for further innovations, for better solutions to the problem of serving the customer well.

We need that same kind of daring idea-generation—teams who allow the community to shape their programs and their methods, rather than a proscribed institutional formula.

Doctrine and personal character remain essential and unchanged, but those man-made systems that quench the Spirit must be reformed. And we need men and women who are brave enough to try new things, who are willing to follow in the footsteps of the Apostle Paul, who said, "I have become all things to all people so that by all possible means I might save some" (1 Corinthians 9:19-23).

These shifts I mentioned a few moments ago will prepare you for the Church Planting Pathway, a framework to release movements, not restrict them.

In chapter 7, I want to address what makes the Church Planting Pathway so unique. And then, in chapter 8, I'm going to lay out the entire system. We will discuss its steps, showing how we plant churches that endure and multiply, so that you can do the same thing in your community.

KEY TAKEAWAYS

- **Jesus' Model:** He started with misfits like Peter and Andrew, teaching them to fish for souls—your harvest team begins with you and Jesus, growing from the field, not pews (Matthew 4:19).

- **Myth Busted:** You don't need an elite team; evangelism and baptisms have declined sharply (Lifeway/Barna, Wagner), as professionalization prioritizes numbers over souls.

- **Harvest Team Reality:** Build from the harvest for credibility and connection (Mike's story in Vermont); importing "experts" falters without cultural fit.

- **Solo Danger:** No one carries the harvest alone—Jesus chose twelve imperfect disciples (John 15:5); shared burdens thrive, lone heroes burn out.

- **Institutional Trap:** Systems like assessments and funding stifle movement (Southern Alberta's forty planters capped at six); shift to Faithfulness-Based Resourcing, Advice/Counsel, harvest-centric models, and equipping for multiplication.

- **Build Your Team:** Use the 3 Ls—Locate (go where people are), Listen (hear their stories: Proverbs 18:13), Love (Christ in you: Galatians 2:20)—then Lean on the Spirit for timing.

- **Your Challenge:** Pray for one harvest team member this week; practice the 3 Ls in your community—start crossing the chasm. Share your first step with me at the QR code below:

Chapter 7

What's Unique About The Church Planting Pathway

"Behold, I do a new thing..."
—Isaiah 43:19

We, those of us who follow Jesus, say we are committed to what Jesus commanded in the Great Commission, yet, so often, we're very far from actually living out or leading our people to follow His commission. To follow Jesus and begin multiplying disciples takes much more shifting and work than most realize. Are you willing to make the shifts it will take to truly obey what He commanded his followers, and especially His leaders, to be about?

Most Christian leaders have not stopped long enough to consider that they are not fulfilling the Great Commission like they may think they are. Or, they have not made a commitment to lead in such a way that their churches are fulfilling Jesus' ultimate commands and requests. This is WHY the American and Canadian church is dying. We must refocus, re-shift, and come back to Jesus' desires for His church.

Can you stop and read that paragraph again? Are you curious about how you may or may not be following what Jesus commanded? If you were living out and leading your church into the great commission, what would you be doing? To be cliché, what did Jesus model for us? What was His *modus operandi* (MO)?

Zacchaeus, a head tax collector despised in Jericho, climbs a sycamore tree, yearning for a glimpse of Jesus. Jesus pauses, looks up, and declares, "Zacchaeus, come down—I must stay at your house today" (Luke 19:5).

Jesus' MO? He saw those who were searching, ready to meet Him, but no one else was even considering or looking for them. This is your calling as a church planter, pastor, or Christian leader: to see the overlooked, the "harvest" as Jesus called them, and guide them into God's Kingdom.

The Church Planting Pathway is a Spirit-led journey to plant and lead churches that focus on the harvest and the multiplying of new disciples. These harvesting and disciple-making churches truly begin to see transformed communities, transformed lives, and the advance of Jesus Christ's mission, which de-populates hell (Luke 19:10).

Let me ask you: Would you give your life, your best of all you have, for what you just read in the paragraph above?

You would probably assume that every Christian organization's plan is to do the same, right? However, with the church in such radical decline in North America, it is obvious that most Christian organizations and even denominations are far from living out what Jesus commanded. Most church leaders, churches, and Christian organizations must see radical shifts… shifts leading us back to Jesus' MO. The Church Planting Pathway is specifically designed for this purpose.

Unlike rigid, one-size-fits-all methodologies–standard assessments with fixed, rigid styles and models, this Pathway bends to the harvest before you and the specific and unique vision Jesus gives to His unique planters.

If you are familiar with church planting and the language of typical church planting culture (at least what has become typical in North America), you will notice some words, phrases, and practices that seem to be missing in the Church Planting Pathway. These are left out intentionally.

Current Methods Make Church Planting Very Slow

Our current method of church planting is MUCH SLOWER than it needs to be. We need strategies that accelerate growth rather than restrict it. Most, if not all, of our current systems are considered effective by the denominations, churches, and organizations that use them. Yet many more churches are dying than are being planted, and more and more people are lost while we pat ourselves on the back.

Clearly, there is a disconnect between what they are measuring and what the world around them is actually experiencing. To get to the root of this issue, we need to consider some of the current church planting language, our common lingo, and recognize that, while we may be saying similar words, we do not appear to be speaking the same language. Yet.

Common Church Planting Language

Assessment: Almost all church planting assessments focus on "key characteristics" of "successful" church planters. The Pathway does not utilize typical assessments or assessment centers. The Church Planting Pathway builds into the planter many of Jesus' core intentions for His church. You will notice in the Pathway that we "affirm" each planter is living out the core purposes of the step of the pathway they are in. If they are not experiencing or living out the core purpose, we do not move them on to the next step in the Pathway until they are fulfilling the key purpose(s) of the Pathway they are in. We wait until they are fulfilling the key purpose(s) of the pathway before we move them to the next step. We "assess" planters and churches on a step-by-step basis with our affirmation process.

Coaching: Most church planting organizations and denominations require church planters to have a coach. Coaches have been very helpful to church planters, but there is a vast shortage of coaches for the amount of church planting being done currently. Thus, there will be an even greater shortage for the amount that actually NEEDS to be done.

The Church Planting Pathway does not utilize coaches. Our Pathway suggests that planters need advice and counsel to lead effectively. Thus, each planter in the Pathway is provided godly counsel and advice regularly, purposefully, and on an as-needed basis from a variety of godly leaders. There is a shortage of people who can coach church planters, but there are many leaders who can give godly counsel, advice, and Biblical wisdom.

Training: This word bothers us the least, but we prefer the word "equip" as it is what we want our church planters to be doing: equipping new believers for future ministry (Ephesians 4:11-12). Why not use as much Biblical language as possible, right? So, we equip our planters in a variety of ways using a variety of tools.

Money: Typical church planting groups that give financial resources to planters give a set amount of resources on a decreasing scale. And normally, a timeline is set when the planter is expected to have funding coming in from the church plant and/or the support raising they have been doing. The phrase we love to use is "faithfulness-based resourcing."

When our planters are faithful with what has been requested of them we give them more resources (Luke 16:10-12). This is why we call our resourcing "faithfulness-based." Financial support is not our only aspect of resourcing. We provide a variety of additional training and books to each planter as they make their way through the Pathway.

The Myth: A Formula Secures Success

Many planters and most church planting organizations believe a standardized formula— funding at some level, a strategic locale, a replicated model, or a standard system of recognizing planters who will succeed—ensures a thriving church. To be clear, this formula is failing. A 2019 Pew Research Center study shows 65% of Americans rarely attend church services, up from 59% a decade prior[26]. A mere 6% may not seem like

---

26   Pew Research Center, "In U.S., Decline of Christianity Continues at Rapid Pace," October 17, 2019, https://www.pewresearch.org/religion/2019/10/17/in-u-s-decline-of-christianity-continues-at-rapid-pace/.

much, but that is almost 2 million people! Barna Group finds 60% of all church plants fail within five years, often because planters impose strategies misaligned with their community's context[27].

The Church Planting Pathway is an alternative to standardized, inflexible formulas. The Pathway grounds you in principles and practices that are flexible and adaptable. Flexible enough to heed the Spirit's leading, ensuring your church takes root in the culture it desires to reach.

How The Church Planting Pathway Creates Momentum

The Pathway is also a relational process with the planter. The planters' specific gifts, their vision from God, the timeline they need, and the culture they are in are all a part of the Planting Pathways flexibility. Imagine a planting pathway that is hyper-flexible to meet the context of the planter and those who so desperately need the Gospel.

This flexibility is greatly needed for several reasons:

North America continues to welcome new people from around the world.

Every planter begins at a different level of experience.

Communities and niche people groups of all shapes and sizes and interests need different types of churches and approaches to church.

---

27   Barna Group, "State of the Church 2021," Barna, 2021, https://www.barna.com/research/state-of-the-church-2021/.

I have watched as multiple ethnic leaders have entered traditional church planting systems and assessments. Unintendedly, English as a second or third language planters were misunderstood and given a lesser church planting assessment outcome for their readiness to plant. I have watched talented, God-called planters be misjudged and driven to question their fit with the organization assessing them and/or they questioned their calling when they are being assessed through a "one-size-fits-all" professional assessment system.

I know a man, a third-language English speaker, who poured his heart into a sample sermon, only to be told it fell short by a committee of church administrators, more focused on his eloquence than his anointing, his calling. With at least 50% or so of new churches needing to speak languages other than English, we must be using very personalized and adaptable systems if we do not want to be missing 50% of the North American population.[28]

Discerning Your Call

Before stepping into the Church Planting Pathway, you must discern: Are you called to plant/pastor? Ask yourself: Am I called to lead people into the harvest? The Church Planting Pathway begins by confirming the planter/pastor's calling, focusing on character and doctrine rather than "success-based" and somewhat peripheral qualifications. As Paul outlines in 1 Timothy 3, a godly leader must be above reproach (be such a good person that no one can rightly criticize them) and be

---

28   Lifeway Research, "The State of Church Planting in Diverse Communities," June 15, 2021, https://research.lifeway.com/2021/06/15/the-state-of-church-planting-in-diverse-communities/.

faithful in their personal life, because integrity undergirds influence. Doctrinal alignment—agreement on salvation, Scripture, and the Gospel—ensures unity.

Many organizations prioritize less critical factors, such as public speaking skills or financial acumen, sidelining the essentials. We've (unfortunately) grown adept at disqualifying people or at least, at highlighting "skills needed" over the commands of Jesus. Instead, the Church Planting Pathway adopts a posture of affirmation, seeking to restore and equip those who are called, even those with imperfect pasts. Remember, before Jesus revealed Himself to the apostle Paul, Paul was actively persecuting early Christians, even having some killed.

We can give you some clear steps to know and understand your calling.

KEY TAKEAWAYS

- **Jesus' Mode of Operation:** He sought the overlooked like Zaccheaus (Luke 19:5), modeling harvest focus—your calling is to do the same, not chase programs or polished services.

- **Myth Busted:** One-size-fits-all formulas fail the harvest (65% non-attenders; 60% plants fail), as rigid systems ignore context and slow momentum.

- **Momentum Through Flexibility:** The Pathway adapts to your culture, experience, and community—hyper-personalized for New Americans/Canadians and diverse needs, unlike traditional one-size-fits-all approaches.

- **Language Shifts:** Ditch "assessment" for affirmation (step-by-step faithfulness); "coaching" for Advice/Counsel (abundant wisdom); "money" for Faithfulness-Based Resourcing (four increases, matching funds); "training" for equipping (movement-oriented, multilingual).

- **Harvest-Centric Over Model-Centric:** Prioritize souls over launches—pour energy into evangelism, not stages, for fruit that lasts (John 15:16).

- **Discerning Your Call:** Focus on character and doctrine, not skills—affirm the called, even from broken pasts, and seek emerging leaders expectantly (1 Timothy 3).

Pause and Act: What "one-size-fits-all" myth is holding you back? Pray Isaiah 43:19 for God's new thing in your context. Reach out at the QR code below to discern your call—let's walk the Pathway together.

Chapter 8

The Church Planting Pathway

"Therefore go and make disciples of all nations..."
–Matthew 28:19

Picture Zacchaeus, a tax collector nobody wanted in Jericho, perched in a sycamore tree, desperate for a glimpse of Jesus. Outcast and overlooked, he's the last soul you'd expect God to chase. Yet Jesus stops, calls him down, and changes his life forever (Luke 19:5). That's the heart of your calling, planter: to seek the lost and spark revival. I've seen too many churches miss this, chasing systems over souls.

The Church Planting Pathway is our Spirit-led answer—a six-step journey to plant churches that don't just stand but multiply disciples, transform communities, and burn for God's harvest. Let's dive into this framework and get moving.

The Six Steps: The Church Planting Pathway

As the Church Planting Pathway unfolds in six steps—Introduction, Follow, Multiply, Team, Launch, Health—each is a milestone toward a harvest-focused, thriving church. I've witnessed their clarifying ability. Let's walk through them together.

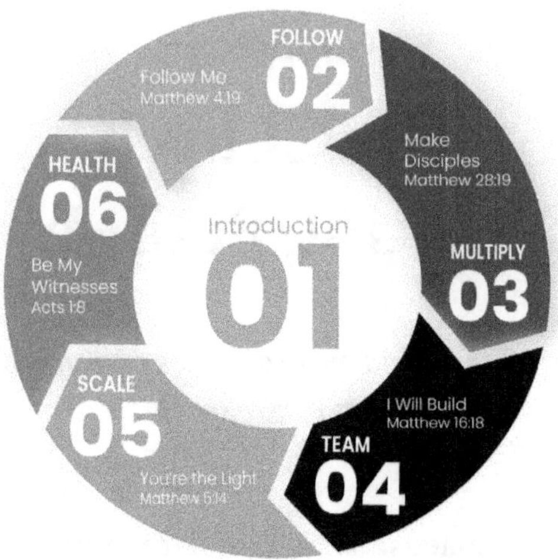

(The above cycle is the Church Planting Pathway we use in the Alliance New England District to show our church planting steps. I wrote this out of my experience of helping a few hundred planters to plant new churches.)

Step 1: Introduction

Let's introduce ourselves to one another, your team, and mine. It is in this step that we learn as much as we can about one another through personal conversation. No initial personality test, just pure conversation. We explain what is important to our group, what we value, and what our vision is, and we also learn the same things about this new potential leader. Then, in our application process, we focus on two main things:

character and doctrinal agreement. That's just about it. We build a relationship and focus on what really matters.

Purpose: The clear purpose here is to discern if you're the right planter for the mission and for you to show us you're the right leader as you review our doctrine, find agreement with it, and we check your character through multiple character references. We also make sure you align with our vision and that you understand what it means to join our movement.

Here in this step called introduction we also explain the six essentials you will experience as you walk in steps 2-6 of the Church Planting Pathway. Let's take a moment to explain the six essentials here.

What You Will Experience: The Essential Elements

All planters experiencing the Church Planting Pathway will find that each step has six essential elements operating within each one.

Here is the way we picture the Essential Elements in the Church Planting Pathway:

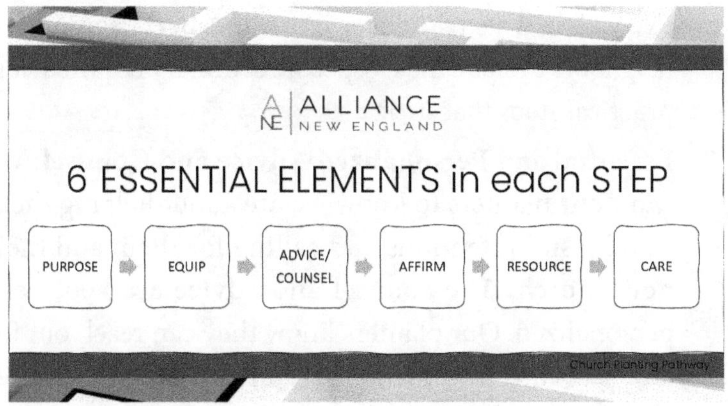

Here is a brief explanation of each of these six elements, drawn from years of walking with planters like you:

1. **Clear Purposes:** We want all of our planters to know what the essential purposes are for the Pathway step they are in. No guessing games. At the start of each step, we lay it out plain: What's God asking you to focus on here? For example, in the Follow step (step 2), the purpose is clear—become a fisher of men, seeking the lost with Jesus' compassion (Matthew 4:19). It's not vague; it's laser-focused on fruit that lasts. I've seen planters flounder without this clarity, chasing shadows. With it, they lock in and see lives change.

2. **Practical Equipping:** Practicality is found in every key point of the equipping we do. We're not dumping theory on you; we're handing you tools you can use tomorrow. Think Bible Discovery Groups (chapter 10) or the 3 Ls (chapter 4)—simple, reproducible steps to reach people right where they are. In the Multiply step (step 3), equipping means training facilitators, not preachers, so almost anyone can lead a group that sparks faith. I've watched a shy rancher in rural Alberta equip their neighbors to share the Gospel; no seminary required, just practical steps that stick.

3. **Essential and Personalized Advice and Counsel:** We want our planters to know we are about helping them fulfill Jesus' intentions and calling for them and their new church. The counsel and advice are kept very personalized. Our planters know they can reach out for any "just-in-time" questions they may have. No one-size-

fits-all. If you're in a hockey-crazy town like Montreal, we won't push a baseball model—we'll advise on what resonates (chapter 5). In the Team step (step 5), counsel might mean tweaking your harvest team to fit your vision. I've had planters text me at midnight, "What do I do with this setback?" and we've turned it into a breakthrough. That's real advice, tailored to your soil.

4. **Affirm Faithfulness:** What faithfulness are we affirming? The planter's faithfulness to the clear purposes we have given them. We celebrate the small wins—the first conversation, the first disciple—because God sees the heart (1 Samuel 16:7). In the Scale step (step 5), affirmation isn't about crowds; it's about asking the question: How do we spread the Gospel message to a larger audience? We want to help you reach as many people as possible. You're not alone—God's affirming you, too.

5. **Faithfulness-Based Resourcing:** As the planter proves faithful to what they have been asked to do (the purpose in each step), we increase our resourcing to them and their plant. The current pathway has four funding increases, including a set amount, matching dollars given for a set amount of dollars raised, as well as two financial grants to assist as the church grows. No blank checks at the start; no cutoffs that leave you hanging. In the Health step (step 6), resourcing means matching funds for a daughter church, fueling multiplication. I've seen a planter go from $100 to full support in a year because he stayed faithful to disciple-making. It's God's way— "faithful with little, entrusted with much" (Luke 16:10).

6. **Planter and Family Care:** We work diligently to care for our planters and the planter's spouse (if married) through prayer, connections, and gatherings, as well as a vacation stipend, insurance assistance, and retirement. Planting's a marathon, not a sprint—burnout's real. In the Follow step (step 2), care might mean a retreat to recharge; in Health (step 6), it's ongoing support for your family. Sue and I have hosted planters for coffee, prayed through crises, and even covered a gap in insurance. It's holistic—your marriage, kids, soul. I've seen families thrive because we prioritized this; neglect it, and the harvest suffers.

These essential elements aren't just supports—they're the wind in your sails, making the Pathway a living partnership with Jesus. As you look to build your harvest team, seek out those emerging leaders who are often overlooked. The church must continually call out yet more planters, as pastoral retirements outpace their replacements, often leaving congregations adrift. We watch expectantly, trusting God to raise laborers for the harvest.

Step 2: Follow—Becoming Fishers of Men

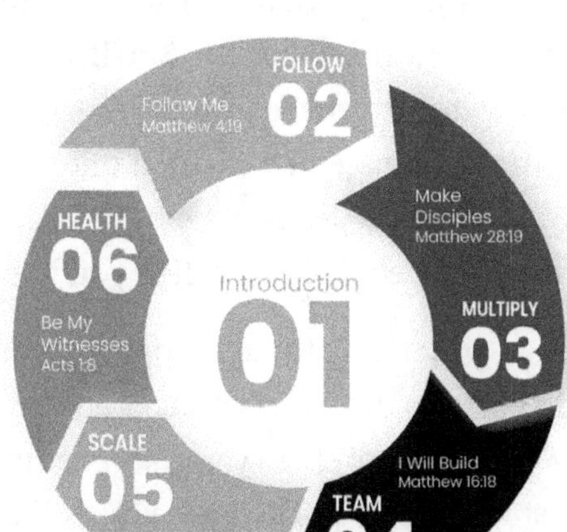

Step 2 of the Church Planting Pathway takes you back to Jesus' first encounters with some of His very first followers. We want you to hear His words and to have an overwhelming desire to follow Him…listen as He says to you, "Follow me, and I will make you fishers of men" (Matthew 4:19). As you commit to follow Him, He begins to form more and more of His heart in you and you realize you are becoming like Him as you are working with Him "to seek and save the lost" (Luke 19:10).

A planter/pastor/Christian leader should carry this heartbeat everywhere they go. This means engaging people in their daily lives, not waiting for their arrival at church. Forget memorized scripts—the Church Planting Pathway leans on the 3 Ls from chapter 4: Locate, Listen, Love—rather than formulaic approaches. Find their places in barbershops, the grocery store, shelters, and soccer fields. Listen to their experiences and, through the Spirit's guidance, discern their fears, their hopes, and dreams. Notice what the Spirit whispers to you, helping you know how to share Jesus with them. Love them through meaningful engagement: with a question, a coffee, a moment of presence. Like Jesus pausing for Zacchaeus, you enter the world of the people Jesus called you to reach.

Training here is practical, focused on authentic Gospel-sharing: how to listen to the Spirit's nudges and how to listen to the person, as well as how to share your faith naturally, and how to pray on the spot. (You'll quickly find yourself introducing a lost person to Jesus in the toilet paper aisle of your local dollar store, or praying for your waitress at the mom-and-pop diner with the huge burgers.)

Step 2 of the Church Planting Pathway invites you to start with a harvest team—two or three who share your passion, hopefully with people you've recently led to Jesus. Why? Typically, new Christ-followers have friends who are not yet following Jesus, and they will introduce you to them and you can help them share the Gospel with their friend circle.

Purpose: The core purpose is to become a fisher of men (Matthew 4:19) and embody Jesus' compassion for the lost (Luke 19:10)—seek them where they are, not where they're not.

Training: Hands-on equipping includes tools like the *3 Ls* and Gospel-sharing guides, so you can start conversations and pray on the spot, turning everyday encounters into divine opportunities.

Advise: Personalized counsel helps you discern the Spirit's nudges in your specific context, like adapting to a barbershop chat or a diner prayer, ensuring your outreach resonates.

Affirm: We affirm your faithfulness to show up and listen, celebrating every step—like your first harvest team member— as God forms Christ's heart in you.

Resource: Initial support provides simple tools (e.g., prayer guides, conversation starters, and Discovery Bible Group scripts) to fuel your first outreaches without overwhelming you.

Care: We work to begin to care for your spouse here in this step and invite them into a network of other spouses for prayer support and relationship. We also pray for you as the planter regularly, and we begin to walk with you as a spiritual father (1 Corinthians 4:15).

Step 3: Multiply—Raising Disciple-Makers

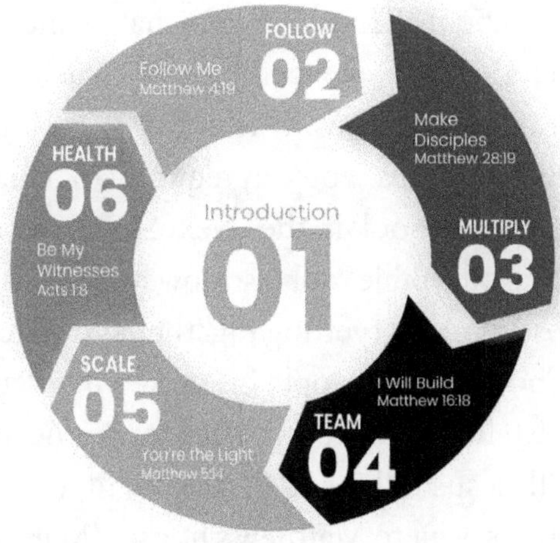

We tend to envision a massive crowd when we read Matthew 28:18-20. A hillside full of people listening intently to the risen Savior. But, if I could take you back to when Jesus first uttered these words, would you find 200 people, 50 people? No, actually, Jesus first uttered these words to the eleven (Judas was not there). When you are utilizing the Church Planting Pathway, you will now be moving into step 3 having begun to lead people to Christ and having at least one baptism. Heaven celebrated this, and so do we! Big time!

Now, in step 3, we want to see disciples multiplied:

> Go out and make disciples in all the nations. Ceremonially wash them through baptism in the name of the triune God: Father, Son, and Holy Spirit. Then disciple them. Form them in the practices and postures that I have taught you, and show them how to follow the commands I have laid down for you. And I will be with you, day after day, to the end of the age." (Matthew 28:19-20)

We get excited about all kinds of ways that planters and pastors can begin helping people to facilitate (not teach, but facilitate) pre-believer types of groups. One of our preferred methods is Discovery Bible Groups (you can request DBG materials from us in the back of the book in the "Next Steps" section for free). These groups are for Bible rookies. However, we also love Alpha groups, Chosen groups (getting together and watching the TV show, The Chosen, with people interested in or curious about Jesus). We also love Matthew parties for connecting not-yet-believers with Jesus followers (You're right, the name comes from when Jesus went to Matthew's house) (Matthew 9:10-13).

In Step 3, we have begun our first financial resourcing for our planters. Why? Because the Scriptures say, 10 If you're faithful in small-scale matters, you'll be faithful with far bigger responsibilities (Luke 16:10). Another translation states: "Whoever can be trusted with small things can also be trusted with big things" (Luke 16:10 ERV).

Since our planters have clear purposes, they know what they are to be about. And we reward their faithfulness. It's the first of four funding increases.

We now want the planter to begin raising up facilitators. Why? We want to see if the planter is able to raise up and equip other people for serving, ministering, and especially for being part of also sharing the Gospel (Ephesians 4:11-13). We watch the planter do this, and we affirm that they are building this key skill of raising disciple-makers and people to serve along with them. We have called this team that is assisting them in the harvest their Harvest team.

All six elements are about supporting the key purpose of multiplication. The multiplication of disciples and raising up new Christ followers to multiply. In this step, we also assist the planter in scheduling prayer retreats for themselves and their team, we help them identify their core values, and as well as help them write a prospectus (we literally give them a "fill in the blank" prospectus so to speak so we can keep them busy harvesting not worrying about a flashy prospectus), and much more.

One thing I admire about the church-planting support we give through the New England District of the Christian and

Missionary Alliance is our unique approach to funding. In many other church-planting support programs I've experienced, the financial resources necessary for a young church to grow are time-based and front-loaded, and follow the same fixed schedule for every planter.

What do I mean by that? Typically, this is the scenario: You're a new church planter and you're moving to a new area with your family. The church planting support network commits to monthly financial support of you and your family, as you focus on building your church, for the first three years, with a fixed percentage decrease each year, and then dropping to zero at the end of the third year. The expectation is that you are simultaneously building a congregation who will tithe and give to the church, which will offset the annual decrease.

But is that how most new churches, built out of the harvest, actually start? No. In reality, when you begin reaching new people for the Kingdom of God, many will first arrive at the church doors with their own financial needs front and center, not at all ready to tithe into the church's Kingdom work. First, you have to help them change their values and beliefs about money. This takes time. However, in the church planting pathway, as you reach more people and prove faithful to the purposes given, you are given more. Systems that decrease over time can quickly drive a planter to get as many tithers as possible, so there will be sufficient resources rather than focusing on building and establishing a church in and out of the harvest.

Purpose: The core purpose is to multiply disciples (Matthew 28:19-20), turning conversions into groups that grow the Kingdom, not just fill rooms.

Equipping: Hands-on equipping includes tools like Discovery Bible Groups (DBG) for Bible rookies, Bible studies like the *Alpha* or *Chosen* series for pre-believers, and Matthew Parties for connecting lost people with believers—reproducible ways to form facilitators, not teachers. We also equip you in writing your values and give you a "plug and play" framework for your church plant, also known as a "prospectus." This is a three to four page document that describes what makes your church plant unique, your geographic area, and the team strategy you've developed.

Advise: Personalized counsel helps you schedule prayer retreats for vision, identify core values (values that shape your ministry and your people, not just a poster on the wall), and craft a simple prospectus ("fill in the blank") to keep you harvesting, not paperwork bound.

Affirm: We affirm your faithfulness to raise facilitators and multiply groups, celebrating skills like equipping others (Ephesians 4:11-13), because God honors obedience.

Resource: First funding increase (modest support) rewards your desire to be in the harvest (Luke 16:10), plus tools for groups, fueling your early fruit.

Care: In this step, we add to the care we were giving before your entrance into our church planter cohorts, so you have a small group of other planters walking with you, praying with you, and supporting you on a peer-to-peer level.

Step 4: Team—Build a Team that Matches the Vision

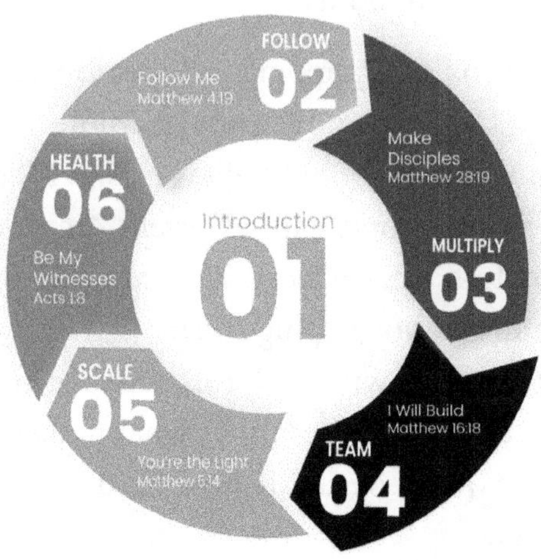

Chapter 6 unpacked the harvest team—those drawn from the field to reach the lost.

As a pastor builds out a new or existing church by using the Pathway, in Step 4, we give you advice and counsel on building the team for the vision that God has given to you as the leader. This is the main purpose of this step.

Let's unpack that for a moment…It is not the organization's or network's job to tell you, the planter, the type of church you need to plant. It is the planter's job to seek from the builder of the church (Jesus) His unique vision for this particular church in this particular location and for a particular culture or people or even a small niche of people. This is why we ask for planters to have prayer retreats, and it's a key part of our

Church Planting Essentials training outcomes. We want you to hear from the builder of the church Himself (Matthew 16:18).

Once the vision is clear, the planter in this step begins to build a team. However, that can be quite daunting and time-consuming. This step gives the planting pastor key advice to share the weight of team building with another team member rather than just themselves. We help the planter find a team mobilizer. This person's role is to engage, recruit, and train others to serve. This helps the pastor to be able to focus on the plant's continued work in the harvest.

At this point, we hope to affirm that the planter and their team will be equipped to build more teams that can accomplish the vision they have received from Jesus. As a result of their faithfulness, resources will increase again and bring yet more support to the new plant and the church planter.

Purpose: The main purpose is to build a team aligned with Jesus' unique vision for your church (Matthew 16:18), ensuring every role serves the harvest and your community's needs.

Equipping: We especially come alongside you in this step to equip you in finding and developing a *team mobilizer*. Believe me, you will thank us for this!

Advise: Personalized counsel helps you find a team mobilizer to share the load, recruiting and training others, so you can stay in the harvest while the team grows. We also continue to advise you on the embedding of your values, and we introduce you to "Safe Place" so that you can protect the children, youth, and families God brings to your church.

Affirm: We affirm your faithfulness to raising up team members and your ability to equip your team, and we love celebrating your continued work in the harvest and the disciple-makers and the team members you are now equipping (Ephesians 4:11-13).

Resource: Second funding increase supports team-building and tools to mobilize others.

Care: We continue all we have done before, and now we do a simple marital assessment to make sure your marriage is staying healthy, so you can also lead a healthy and growing ministry.

Step 5: Scale—Shining as a Beacon

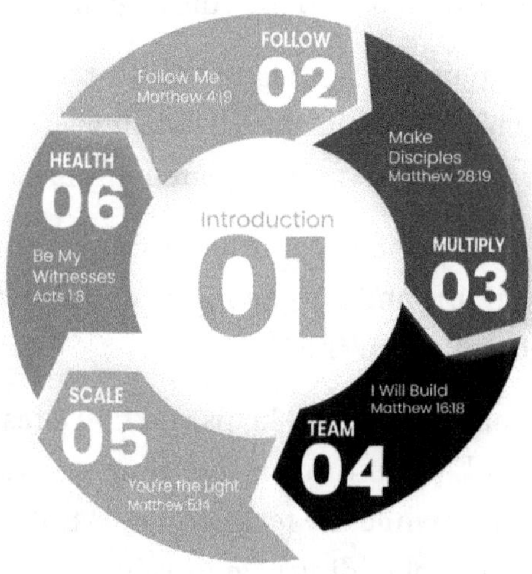

Jesus described His followers this way, "And you, beloved, are the light of the world. A city built on a hilltop cannot be hidden" (Matthew 5:14). Step 5 of the Pathway prepares your church plant to shine brighter and brighter, not with hype but rather with clarity.

We clarify:

1. Scaling the team: What team members and leaders/facilitators do you need to keep scaling?

2. Scaling ministries: What ministries are needed now to keep scaling toward the vision you have?

3. Launch team needs, if this will be a launch-style type of plant. If it will be more of a house church or small group cell, then we focus on the needs of the facilitator or group leaders.

4. Social media needs.

5. Giving strategies.

As you can see, we walk with you as the planter and pastor in many more ways than this list as well. We are working with you toward your final increase in your financial resourcing when you complete this step. We have helped you work toward your second funding grant in this step, as you will need more resources to keep scaling. We have also increased our matching grant toward you in this stage so we can match more funds that are coming in from the hard work of fund raising a planter will do.

This scaling is not about mere visibility, a marketing campaign for your first church services, but rather a bold proclamation of God's Kingdom. A radical way of being rather than just doing. Consider one of our planters who took me on a hike on the

Appalachian Trail in New Hampshire. As we hiked, he directed our group to pray for the people we met along the way. Not silently, but actually asking them if we could pray for them. Only one person turned us down. And we shared the Gospel a few times as well. He is modeling and building out a team that will meet people in multiple ways throughout the region their church plant is called to serve.

Purpose: To scale as a "city on a hill" (Matthew 5:14), clarifying teams, ministries, and strategies to boldly proclaim God's Kingdom in ways that resonate with your community.

Equipping: Hands-on equipping for scaling includes training on team expansion, ministry development, and giving strategies, so you can grow without losing harvest focus.

Advise: Personalized counsel clarifies scaling needs (e.g., social media for your niche, launch team for your vision), helping you adapt to your community's pulse.

Affirm: We affirm your faithfulness to scale boldly, celebrating milestones like your first prayer-on-the-trail Gospel share.

Resource: Third funding increase (second grant) and expanded matching supports scaling (e.g., ministry tools, social media setup), rewarding and supporting your bold proclamation.

Care: We offer prayer and family check-ins as scaling accelerates, ensuring relational health amid expansion. Our planters know they can count on us for "just in time" prayer support. We receive numerous prayer requests every week, and we stand boldly with our leaders on the front lines of ministry!

The Pathway balances urgency with readiness, affirming your progress while advising on team development. Like Jesus sending the seventy-two disciples, you go as He requests, carrying His message to those awaiting hope, an ever brighter and shining light expanding into the darkness, saving more and more who were once lost in that darkness (Luke 10:1).

Step 6: Health—Multiplying the Harvest

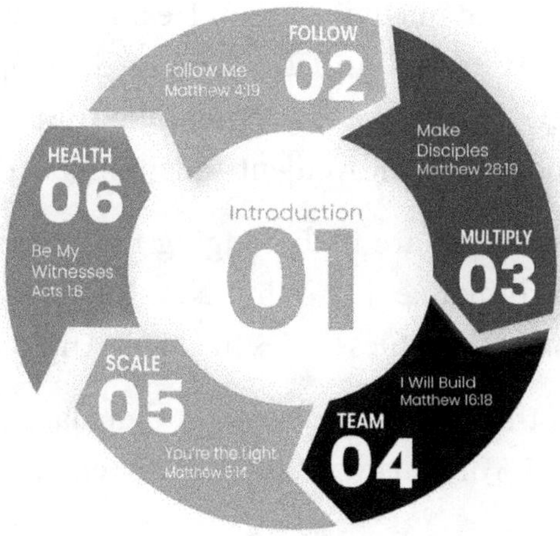

Now, it's time to address the health of your newly established (or newly invigorated) church. Its Health lies not in number of participants but rather in the expanding of the Kingdom of God through prayerfully and intentionally developing new disciples, groups, and even more churches in other areas. This can even include a focus on subcultures within your current community. Ever imagine you might reach your local skateboarding subculture? What about the group of Nigerian refugees across town? What about a different city, a different country, maybe even an as-yet-unreached people group?

Our main Scripture behind this step in the Pathway is Acts 1:8.

"Here's the knowledge you need: You will receive power when the Holy Spirit comes on you. And you will be My witnesses, first here in Jerusalem, then beyond to Judea and Samaria, and finally to the farthest places on earth" (Acts 1:8).

Step 6 equips planters and pastors to foster movements and to continue to build the dynamics of Health. These dynamics include healthy teams and leadership development, so the church mothering the movement continues to lay the foundations needed for movement and multiplication.

In New England, we are truly longing for more and more churches that think like this. Why? New England is home to some of the most churchless cities in North America.

Churches like this are sorely needed in Canada, as well. As of 2021, almost 35% of Canadians claimed no religious affiliation at all[29].

Purpose: To embody Acts 1:8 as a healthy, multiplying church. We envision you knowing at this point your next planting location and you have raised up at least one pastor, church planter, or even your takeover pastor, so you can move on and plant and lead again!

---

29   Statistics Canada, "Religion by Indigenous identity, age group and sex," 2021 Census of Population, October 26, 2022, https://www12.statcan.gc.ca/census-re-censement/2021/dp-pd/prof/details/page.cfm?Lang=E&SearchText=religion&D-GUID=2021A000011124&Gender=1&StatProv=01&Header=1.

Equipping: Leadership development training equips you to mentor multipliers, fostering healthy teams and foundations for ongoing movement. We equip you specifically in this by having you attend a training entitled: Healthy Church Dynamics by DCPI (Dynamic Church Planting International).

Advise: Personalized counsel on subcultures (e.g., skateboarding, refugees) and expansion (e.g., new cities), as well as advise on continued team development, and we review your Healthy Church Dynamics Implementation plan.

Affirm: We affirm your faithfulness to multiply, celebrating new groups or plants as signs of Kingdom expansion.

Resource: We now see financial resources as a conversation. Even though we do not have "cut-off dates" for funding, we do expect that you and your team have begun to raise more and more support for the church. Our conversation stems from what resources you need at that point. We also apply for resources and equip you so you can become a "greenhouse" church, so you can continue to raise up more and more new leaders.

Care: Ongoing family and team care, including retreats and connections, sustains health as multiplication accelerates.

This step envisions a legacy beyond the walls of your own church planting and pastoring assignment. A healthy church raises leaders who plant again, like ripples from a stone tossed into a pond. Training emphasizes reproduction (mentorship-teaching you to guide others as you were guided), while Advising ensures you stay outward focused. Resources can support the raising up of new leaders that will sustain this vision, while Affirmation celebrates Acts 1:8 advancement. Care remains vital, guarding your spirit as you pour into others, along with caring for your spouse and family.

Multiplication requires sacrifice, not comfort. The Pathway challenges you to release control, trusting God's Spirit to carry the mission forward. As Paul planted and Apollos watered, your role is to sow faithfully, knowing God gives the increase (1 Corinthians 3:6). Health transforms your church into a movement, igniting revival across generations and nations.

The Challenge: Step Forward Now

The Church Planting Pathway is not a formula but rather a partnership with Jesus, adaptable to every type of community and flexible enough to follow the winds of the Spirit. Its essential elements—Purpose, Equip, Advise, Affirm, Resource, Care—guide and secure you in every step; taking you from calling to multiplication. Zacchaeus' redemption shows what's possible when you look for, listen to, and love the lost.

We look forward to helping you walk into the Church Planting Pathway. It is your Pathway, your new GPS for being in the Harvest. I would encourage you to walk back through the Pathways points and understand how you can take each step with the greatest of intentionality in the situation you find yourself in. Of course, at the end of the book, you will find many tools, including the Pathway, but we are also glad to talk with you now.

Next, we will explore bearing fruit. Jesus speaks very clearly to us about His expectations for His leaders that he gave right before he went to the cross. It is such a powerful message of His that we will look at and respond to.

I encourage you to step forward, as a planter/pastor called to ignite God's Kingdom into the darkness remembering and being blown away by what He said," I tell you the truth: whoever believes in Me will be able to do what I have done, but they will do even greater things, because I will return to be with the Father (John 14:12).

KEY TAKEAWAYS

- **Seek the Lost Like Jesus:** Zacchaeus shows the heart—see the overlooked, call them down (Luke 19:5), and spark revival; your calling is to chase souls, not systems.

- **Myth Busted:** One-size-fits-all formulas fail the harvest, ignoring context and slowing momentum.

- **Essential Elements:** The six elements—Purpose, Equipping, Advise, Affirm, Resource, Care—weave through every step, providing clarity, tools, guidance, celebration, scaling support, and holistic wellbeing.

- **Discerning Call:** Focus on character and doctrine (1 Timothy 3), not skills (we can grow those), affirm the ones who have been called from their broken pasts, like Javier's redemption, and seek emerging leaders expectantly.

- **Review the Church Planting Pathways Steps:** If you are leading a current ministry, what aspects of the pathway do you need to develop and work on? If you are planting a church, where are you in the Pathway? What do you need

Pause and Act: Which step stirs you most? Pray Isaiah 43:19 for God's new thing in your context. Reach out to discern your call—let's walk the Pathway together. Here is a QR code to make it easier:

Chapter 9

To Bear Fruit

*"I have chosen you...so that you would go and bear fruit
and keep on bearing..."*
–John 15:16

I n Charlie Chaplin's *The Great Dictator*, the Jewish barber steps into the spotlight, delivering a speech that shakes the soul. His plea for peace, empathy, and resistance to tyranny echoes across decades, stirring hearts with its universal cry for humanity to reject hatred and oppression. It's powerful, unforgettable, and resonates throughout generations and across cultures, highlighting the importance of empathy.

But there's a speech far greater, spoken not on a stage but at a humble table, hours before a cross. Jesus, surrounded by His disciples at their final meal, pours out His heart. Here is an excerpt in The Voice translation: "You did not choose Me. I chose you, and I orchestrated all of this so that you would be sent out and **bear great and perpetual fruit** [that's my favorite part!]. As you do this, anything you ask the Father in My name will be done" (John 15:16).

Let's read it again from the Amplified translation. Read it out loud this time for effect, "You have not chosen Me, but I have chosen you and I have appointed and placed and purposefully planted you, so that you would go and bear fruit and keep on bearing, and that your fruit will remain and be lasting, so that whatever you ask of the Father in My name He may give to you" (John 15:16 AMP).

These are Jesus' final words before going to the cross. He is clearly saying why he chose His disciples and even why He has chosen *you* today, for fruit bearing. What is this fruit? It is new disciples. Jesus started His earthly ministry by calling His disciples to fish for men, and He concluded it with a final charge: to go and bear fruit.

Any serious follower of Jesus who is called to serve Him as a church planter, pastor, and Christian leader needs to take Jesus' challenge very seriously. How seriously are you taking this message from Jesus? Really?

I'm begging you to hear this: This message is not meant to be optional. Although with the low level of evangelism taking place, it seems like even Christian leaders feel it is an option. He chose you to follow Him and bear fruit—great, perpetual fruit, lives transformed for eternity. New disciples, anchored in Christ. From the start, He called His disciples to fish for men; now, at the end, He seals it with a command to bear fruit. If you're a church planter, pastor, or leader, this is your calling. Let's unpack what it means to bear fruit that lasts, to hunger for a harvest, and to live the story God is writing through you.

The Myth: Minimal Impact Is Enough

Too many planters settle for a low bar." If just one soul is saved," they say, as if *that's* the goal. I get it. Every person matters. But boy, is that selling God short. "The Lord added to them daily those who were being saved" (Acts 2:47). Daily! Not one here or there, but a movement of people being saved. Yet, some cling to a myth: minimal impact is enough, a trickle of fruit satisfies Jesus' call. But this mindset limits your vision. Ephesians 3:20 promises God can do "exceedingly abundantly above all we ask or think." Why settle for just *one* soul saved when we could see a 100-fold harvest instead?

What Fruit Looks Like

Picture a fertile vineyard, vines heavy with clusters so lush they bow the branches. That's the fruit Jesus envisions. Disciples who make disciples, churches that birth churches, and lives transformed for eternity. Numbers can't tell the whole story, but they're not nothing. In Numbers 13, Caleb and Joshua carried a *single cluster of grapes* so massive it took two men to haul it.

That's the kind of fruit we're after—abundant, undeniable, God-sized. Fruit isn't just baptisms; it's people growing in Christ, families restored, neighborhoods shifted. It's messy, tough, and, let me tell you, it's what makes growing a church so much fun!! When you're reaching people, really reaching them, it's a wild ride. You just have to see it through the right eyes: eyes fixed on the harvest, not the hassle.

Jesus' words are clear: He planted you "purposefully" to bear fruit that "remains and is lasting" (John 15:16). This isn't a one-and-done deal. It's perpetual—disciples who keep multiplying, churches that keep planting. And the promise? "Whatever you ask of the Father in My name, He may give to you." When you're bearing fruit, your prayers align with His mission, and heaven moves. I'm asking God daily to make me a fruit-bearer, not for a pat on the back, but for His glory.

What's He saying to you in this verse? Stop and listen. Let His message sink in.

Hunger for the Harvest

Here's the deal: we don't have the problem of too much harvest. Not even close. We're searching for the *first* fruit here. I'd love the challenge of saying, "What do we do with all these people?!" Wouldn't you?

Don't be scared of the work of finding the harvest. Some churches shy away, worried it'll be too messy, too hard, and then wonder why their ministry efforts stagnate. But that mess? That's where the joy is. "Take up your cross daily" (Luke 9:23). It's not easy, but it's worth it. Get hungry for what bearing fruit looks like—Heaven rejoicing (Luke 15:7), people lost in darkness, literally lost in darkness, found (Isaiah 9:2, Matthew 4:16), and revival sparking. The Lord can do way more than we dream, so why settle for less?

Challenge what you've known and what you've seen in your church or community before. Maybe your experience has been a trickle—a few baptisms, a small group. That's not the ceiling.

The book of Acts shows thousands "were added daily," cities were turned upside down (Acts 2:41, Acts 17:6). We want *that* problem. The beautiful chaos of new disciples piling in. Don't let a low bar from past ministries box you in. God's ready to unleash a harvest if you'll pray for it, work for it, believe for it. And, with godly counsel and advice, you *can* get there.

You knew this was coming… but are you ready to enter the harvest with everything you've got?

A Story of Fruit: George's Story

Remember me telling you about my buddy George earlier in this book? George is a pastor and planter I've known for twenty years. He didn't just plant a church; God transformed an entire community through his harvesting. George's church has discipled hundreds, restored families, and shifted the spiritual landscape of his town.

But George's impact didn't stop there. He also helped start other churches, each bearing fruit of its own, spreading revival like wildfire. *That's* lasting fruit: disciples making disciples, churches planting churches. George's story could be yours. You're not just planting a church; you're igniting a movement. I've seen it happen, and I'm praying it happens through you.

Fruit-bearing isn't about perfection. George faced messes—people's struggles and the weight of his own daily cross. But he kept his eyes on the harvest, and God has done "exceedingly abundantly more" than George and his team could have ever imagined.

The team that is with you right now may be small and just forming, but don't underestimate what God can do. Pray for God to give you more than you could have ever imagined when it comes to people finding Christ! Every step of the Pathway—Follow, Multiply, Team, Scale, and Health—builds toward this. Chapter 7 gave you the map; now, let's hunger for and advance into the harvest.

Your Call to Bear Fruit

This is where it gets real. Jesus didn't *suggest* fruit-bearing; He *commanded* it. "I have chosen you… so that you would go and bear fruit" (John 15:16). That's not a side gig—it's your purpose. Stop right now and pray.

I mean it. Pause here and talk to the Father.

Ask Him to make you a fruit-bearer, not for a little fruit, but for a massive, lasting harvest. Implore Him to let you see people saved, disciples multiplied, and communities changed. Pray like Caleb eyeing Canaan, ready for grapes too big for one man to carry.

It starts with hunger. Get desperate for revival. Don't settle for "one soul saved" when God's ready to add fives, tens, fifties, hundreds, and even thousands. Take up your cross, fish for men, women, youth, and children; watch Him move. I'm urging you: Commit to living a life of fruit-bearing and ignite a movement that lasts.

A Prayer for Revival

The Church Planting Pathway isn't just steps—it's a covenant to bear fruit that glorifies God. Zacchaeus' transformed heart shows what's possible when you answer Jesus' call. I've seen fruit change neighborhoods and communities, and I'm asking God to let you see it too. Don't let this chapter pass you by. Pray again: "Father, make me a fruit-bearer. Give me a harvest that lasts."

Practice the *4* Ls, Locate, Listen, Love, and Lean. Find one person this week, and ask, "God, how can You use me to reach them?"

Step out, Christian leader, and bear fruit that shakes eternity.

KEY TAKEAWAYS

- **Jesus' Final Charge:** Chaplin's speech stirs the soul, but Jesus' words at the Last Supper command you to "bear great and perpetual fruit" (John 15:16):new disciples, lives transformed, lasting for eternity. Read it aloud and let it sink in.

- **Myth Busted:** Minimal impact ("just one soul saved") sells God short; Acts 2:47 shows daily additions; aim for the vineyard's abundance (Caleb's grapes), not a low bar.

- **What Fruit Looks Like:** Disciples making disciples, churches birthing churches—messy, tough, but joyful; see it through harvest eyes, not hassle (Luke 9:23).

- **Hunger for the Harvest:** We lack "too much harvest"— embrace the chaos of souls flooding in; challenge your trickle experiences with "exceedingly abundantly more" (Ephesians 3:20).

- **Prayer Call:** Beg God for massive, lasting fruit—stop and pray now: "Make me a fruit-bearer, not for little, but for a harvest that shakes eternity."

Pause and Act: What low bar are you raising? Pray John 15:16 aloud today. List three "daily additions" goals (e.g., one conversation, one prayer). Share your hunger—let's bear fruit together.

Chapter 10

Critical to the Conversation

*"He must manage his own household well...for if someone
does not know how to manage his own household, how
will he care for God's church?"*
–1 Timothy 3:4-5

When Jesus called His disciples, He didn't hand them a job description with "preach killer sermons" at the top. He said, "Follow Me, and I will make you fishers of men" (Matthew 4:19). That's the heart of a pastor–ot a performer, but a shepherd, a soul-chaser, and a disciple-maker.

As a church planter, you're not just starting a church; you're stepping into a sacred role. Chapter 8 showed you the Church Planting Pathway, which helps you build; chapter 9 challenged you to bear much fruit—new disciples for eternity. Now, we're getting to the core of who you are as a pastor.

We must get this part of the journey right. Too many pastors and church planters have not understood this: The Bible lays out three critical non-negotiables that define a pastor: character, family, and doctrine. Let's unpack what makes a

137

pastor's heart, because this is where your calling lives or dies, and it's only in having these non-essentials right, where you will be able in God's power to see dying churches become dangerous (in an Acts 17:6 kind of way).

The Myth: Skills Make the Pastor

Here's a trap we fall into: thinking a pastor is defined by skills like preaching, leading meetings, or casting vision. Job postings list pages of qualifications, but how many mention evangelizing the lost? I've seen pastoral searches obsess over sermon delivery, while the harvest, people still in the darkness of their sin and separation from God, gets ignored. The myth is that skills make the pastor, that a slick talker equals a godly leader. That's not what the Apostle Paul said when he wrote, "The sermons I preached were not delivered with *the kind of* persuasive elegance *some have come to expect*, but they were effective because I relied on God's Spirit to demonstrate God's power" (1 Corinthians 2:4).

Preaching can be taught, but a heart for salvations has to burn inside you as a pastor. The Bible doesn't care about your stage presence; it demands a life that preaches before you open your mouth. Let's focus on what God says a pastor is, and you can learn the rest.

Character: The Foundation of Leadership

Look at 1 Timothy 3 and Titus 1. These two chapters highlight God's blueprint for leaders. It's not about eloquence or charisma; it's about character. Are you above reproach (your actions and character are such that no one can honestly accuse you of wrongdoing)? Self-controlled? Hospitable? Not a drunk, not greedy, not quick-tempered? These are meant to be the pulse of your life as a minister. Character isn't just what you do; it's who you are when no one's watching.

We can teach you to preach, to plant, to lead. But your heart? That's on you to allow God's Spirit, His word, and men and women of God to shape you.

This has hit me hard over the years. Early on, I thought success was found in packed services and growing student ministries. But God kept pointing me back to my life—how I treated my wife, how I spoke to my kids, how I stewarded myself in the small moments, when no one but God was watching. Ask yourself: Am I *being* the leader God desires to have in spiritual leadership?

Check your character against 1 Timothy 3. That's not a one-time test; it's your daily cross (Luke 9:23). Live so your church and, better yet, your family, sees Jesus in you, not just in your words. That's the pastor's foundation.

Family: Your First Ministry

Here's where I didn't do as well as I should've. Hindsight is always 20/20. The Bible's clear: a pastor's first ministry is their family. 1 Timothy 3:4-5 says, "He must manage his own household well… for if someone does not know how to manage his own household, how will he care for God's church?" Your spouse, your kids—they're your first disciples.

Your family isn't a side project; it's the proving ground for your leadership. Are you discipling your kids with the same zeal you bring to Bible studies? Are you loving your spouse like Christ loves the church (Ephesians 5:25)? I'm not saying it's easy—planting a church is demanding, and there's always a new harvest need. But your church needs to know your family is your top priority. Set boundaries: date nights, family dinners, and prayer time with your kids. Equip your people to honor those boundaries and teach them that a pastor is not a hired hand, but a shepherd who leads at home. When your family thrives, it's a testimony to the Gospel you're planting. Get this wrong, and no amount of fruit will cover the cost.

Doctrinal Agreement: Anchored in Eternity

Doctrine is the third non-negotiable. What matters most for eternity? Salvation by grace through faith, in Christ alone, Jesus' divinity, Scripture's authority—these are the hills to die on. Everything else? Debatable, discussable. I've seen planters get hung up on side issues like worship styles and end-times charts, while the harvest languishes. Here's a pro tip: If it isn't an issue that determines whether or not a person enters Heaven, it's not worth your focus.

These arguments are merely side quests, slowing us down, weighing us down, and they risk alienating the harvest. Make sure the group you're planting with aligns with the essentials. If you're fighting over secondary stuff, you're not fishing for people.

This ties to your heart for the lost. Most job descriptions skip evangelism, but Jesus didn't. He started with "fish for men" and ended with "bear fruit" (Matthew 4:19, John 15:16). A pastor's doctrine has to fuel that mission. Your beliefs should light a fire for the harvest, not a debate club. Check your doctrine against your organization, denomination, network, and church. Agree on what's eternal, then run toward the lost together or find a partnering organization that agrees with doctrines that matter for eternity if the one you are a part of does not.

Your Call to Be a Pastor

This is the conversation we can't skip: A church planter *is* a pastor. And for pastors, God's standard is clear: character, family, doctrine. Not preaching, not programs, not polish. Live with integrity, so your life preaches Christ. Shepherd your family, so your home reflects His love. Hold fast to doctrine, so your mission stays Kingdom-focused. These aren't add-ons; they're the heart of who you are. I've seen planters stumble, not for lack of skills, but for missing this. Let's get it right.

Stop and pray right now. Ask, "Lord, shape my character, guard my family, anchor my doctrine." Ask Him to make you a pastor after His heart, with a fire for the lost. Practice the 3 Ls from chapter 4—Locate, Listen, Love—starting at home. Tell your spouse, "You're my first ministry." Teach your church, "My family's my number 1 assignment."

Remember, you're not just planting a church. You're shepherding souls, starting with your own.

The Pastor's Heart

The Church Planting Pathway is your map; bearing fruit is your responsibility to Jesus' mission, but being a pastor requires *solid* character. George's mission transformed a town; Buck's passion for the souls of the indigenous youth prevented the arrival of tipi-shaking demonic activity. Miracles happen through pastors whose character, families, and doctrine align with Jesus. I've failed at times, but God's grace redeems.

A Story of Grace: My Family's Journey

Let me get real. I didn't always put my family first. Between planting churches, and advancing the Kingdom, I poured so much into the harvest that my wife and kids sometimes got shortchanged. But God's grace is bigger than my failures. Today, I'm so grateful our kids are walking with God, married to spouses who love Jesus. That's not my doing; it's His! And a lot of credit also goes to my amazing wife's investment in our kids. They're my first disciples, and their faith is fruit that lasts.

This isn't just my story. It's yours too. Your family's your first discipling priority. When your kids see you pray, when your spouse feels your love, those are sermons louder than any heard from the pulpit. I'm begging you: Make your family your priority. Equip your church to support this, and you'll plant and pastor something that endures—not just a church, but a legacy of faith.

I'm urging you, fish for men, love your people, and start at home. Pray again: "Father, make me Your shepherd." Find people this week and ask, "God, how can You use me to reach them?" Pastor God's people with a life that echoes into eternity.

KEY TAKEAWAYS

- **Pastor's True Identity:** Jesus called disciples to fish for men (Matthew 4:19), not preach sermons—your role is shepherd, soul-chaser, disciple-maker, not performer.

- **Myth Busted:** Skills like preaching define the pastor, but the Bible demands a heart for salvations (1 Corinthians 2:4). Pastor job postings miss this, chasing polish over passion.

- **Character Foundation:** 1 Timothy 3 and Titus 1 prioritize integrity—above reproach, self-controlled—because your life preaches louder than words; we can teach skills, but character shapes your witness.

- **Family First Ministry:** Your household is your proving ground (1 Timothy 3:4-5)—disciple your spouse and kids with zeal; Gary's hindsight regret shows neglect costs, but grace redeems.

- **Doctrinal Anchor:** Focus on eternal essentials (salvation by grace, Jesus' divinity, Scripture's authority)—side issues like worship styles distract from the harvest.

- **Grace in the Journey:** Gary's family story reminds us: failures don't disqualify; prioritize home to plant a legacy of faith that echoes eternity.

Pause and Act: What non-negotiable (character, family, doctrine) needs your focus most? Pray 1 Timothy 3:4-5 today. This week, disciple one family member with the 3 Ls—locate, listen, love. Share your step at www.thechurchplantingpathway. com—let's shepherd together.

PART 3

Putting It Into Practice

Chapter 11

God Loves People More Than Anything

*"When He saw the crowds, He had compassion for them,
because they were harassed and helpless, like sheep
without a shepherd."*
–Matthew 9:36

Jesus stood on a hillside, gazing at the crowds—broken, wandering, lost. His heart broke for the people He loved more than anything. Not buildings, not programs, not applause, but people adrift, "like sheep without a shepherd" (Matthew 9:36). That's God's heart for you, and it's got to be your heart for the people around you as well.

Part 2 of this book laid out the Church Planting Pathway. Now, in part 3, we're getting practical. It starts with loving people like Jesus does.

Stop for a moment and ask God to break your heart for what breaks His, or rather, for *who* breaks His heart. Now, let's dive into why *people* are God's passion and how you can reach them, because God loves people more than anything.

Our Challenge: Ministry Can Easily Matter More Than People

We love ministry, don't we? Preaching, planting, leading. It's thrilling. But here's the trap: We can sometimes love the *idea* of church planting more than the *people* God sent us to reach. I've seen it, and it's disheartening. You can pack a service, nail a sermon, and still miss the harvest…the people who God loves. The challenge is that many people buy into the false belief that ministry is the goal, or that a slick church plant equals success. That's not Jesus' heart. He wept over Jerusalem (Luke 19:41) and ached for the lost (Matthew 4:19). If your heart is not breaking for people, you're not planting His church. We've got to shift and love people first, because God does. Everything flows from that, and if we don't get that part right, we're just playing church.

God's Heart: Compassion for the Lost

Let me repeat: God loves people more than anything. 1 John 4:8 says, "God is love," and John 3:16 proves it: "For God so loved the world that He gave His only Son." Jesus didn't come for systems or status; He came to die for people. His compassion was gut-wrenching, seeing crowds "harassed and helpless" (Matthew 9:36).

Do you feel this when you see people? If so, that's the compassionate heart of Jesus driving your call. If the mind of Christ dwells in you richly (Colossians 3:16), you'll feel it: a compulsion to seek and save the lost (Luke 19:10). I've watched leaders, like the current president of the Christian and Missionary Alliance, weep on stage, burdened and broken for the unreached. That's not a show; that's God's heart pulsing through him.

Who breaks your heart? A people group? Immigrants in your city? Kids on your street? Name them—specific names, faces, or groups. God's asking you to reach them. Maybe it's Muslims you pass daily, or coworkers who don't know Christ. Whoever they are, your heart's got to ache like Jesus' did. If it doesn't, stop and pray again. Ask, "God, break my heart for what breaks Yours." This isn't optional—it's the fuel for your developing church and for your own heart. Without fuel, we're just gathering, not expanding God's kingdom.

With God's heart for people in mind, let's talk about how we implement the Church Planting Pathway in practical ways. Here are some tips and tools that you can begin implementing immediately.

Practical Steps: Reaching the Lost

Loving people's not just a feeling; it's an action. The Pathway equipped you to fish for people; now, here's how to start. These tools are simple, reproducible, and built for the harvest. Try them today—don't wait.

1. Discovery Bible Groups

One of the best ways to reach people is through Bible Discovery Groups. These are simple gatherings where anyone can explore Scripture. They aren't Sunday school classes or sermons; they're Bible-rookie-led, rookie-attended, non-threatening question-based studies, often in homes or coffee shops. You ask the same clear questions every time, focusing on one paragraph, like from the Gospel of John, which shares Christ's heart so well. The Bible's the teacher; you're just a facilitator (James 3:1). A newbie watches you lead once and thinks, "I could do that." It's free, multilingual, and spreads fast. You don't need a copyright, just go. I've seen these groups spark faith in people who've never opened a Bible.

2. Top 5 Names List

Grab a pen and a sheet of paper. Write down five people you know who don't know Christ. This is your Top 5 Names list. Pray for them daily: salvation, softened hearts, and open doors. I taught this to African planters in Portland, Maine, and Pastor Isaac got fired up. He took it to his church plant where his wife listed five names and got to praying for them immediately. The next day, three of those very people she had listed showed up to their gathering. They then gave their lives to Christ. That's God moving! Praying for people stirs your heart. You can't help it.

Who's on your list? Neighbors? Family? Co-workers? Lift their names to God, and watch Him work.

3. The *3 Ls*: Locate, Listen, Love

In chapter 4, we talked about the 3 Ls—Locate, Listen, Love— to start conversations. Go where people are: parks, workplaces, your neighborhood. Listen to their stories, their pain, and their desires. Love them the way Jesus loves them. Today, have one conversation with someone on your Top 5 list. Ask, "What's your story?" or "How can I pray for you?" It's not a script; as I pointed out in Chapter 7, it's Jesus' way—meeting Zacchaeus where he was (Luke 19:5). These talks plant seeds that have the potential to change a person's life for eternity.

4. The Stakes: Lostness and Eternity

Why the urgency? People are lost. They're not just confused… they're eternally separated from God. Jesus talked about hell more than almost anything, second only to money. It's not popular, but it's inescapable in the New Testament. He warned of "eternal fire" and "outer darkness" because He loves people too much to sugarcoat it (Matthew 25:41, Matthew 22:13). Lostness isn't just this life's struggle; it's being consigned to live out all of eternity, forever, without God.

That's the reality driving your call. If you don't believe people are lost, why pastor a congregation? Why plant a new church? And if you do believe as I do, how can you stay quiet? This truth ought to break your heart. Pray for eyes to see others through the lens of eternity.

5. Stories of the Lost

Pastor Isaac and his wife didn't just pray vaguely—they named five people, prayed earnestly, and invited them to their gathering. Three of those five people showed up and met Jesus. That's what happens when your heart breaks for *specific* souls. It's not theory; it's action.

I have a friend who tells this story: "When I was about eight, living in Michigan, I got in a spat with a friend and ran home crying to my mom. She sat me down and said, 'Suzanne, what you don't understand is that some people have never had their names lifted up before the throne of Christ.'"

Think with me for a moment about that. How many people have never, I mean *never*, been prayed for?

Have you asked, "Has anyone prayed for that person walking by? The woman in a hijab? Or the guy at the gas station?" I might be the first. Pray for the random stranger you see, and God may hear you praying the very first prayer ever prayed for that person. Wow! How profound!

My friend Paul led a group of thirty Chinese tourists into the Canadian Rockies. An hour in, he realized they were lost. No map, no cell phone signal, just wilderness. They continued hiking, the tourists oblivious to their danger, and Paul thought, "I didn't even tell my wife where I was going. She doesn't know where I am." Finally, after several hours, one of their phones caught a signal, and they found a fire road to safety.

But out there, Paul came face to face with a gut-wrenching truth: It's one thing to be lost; it's another to be lost when no one's looking for you.

That's the world we live in. Millions adrift, and no one's searching. Who are you looking for? If we're not, God forgive us. This story's not just Paul's—it's ours, too.

6. Your Call to Reach the Lost

This chapter's not about guilt; it's about God's love. Jesus saw the lost and acted. He died for them. You're called to do the same, in your way, in your city. Stop and pray: "Lord, break my heart for the lost. Show Jesus to your people."

Who is on your Top 5 list? Jot their names down and pray a quick, simple prayer over them. Start a Discovery Bible conversation today. Find one co-worker, or a neighbor, and say,

"Let's read the Gospel of John together." Use the 3 Ls—Locate, Listen, Love. Love people like Jesus does.

They're lost, and you may be the only one looking for them.

Who Are You Looking For?

Pastor Isaac's three people without Christ, Suzanne's mom, and Paul's hikers remind us that people are lost, and God's counting on us to look for them.

Pray again: "Father, show me the lost I need to reach." This week, talk to the people on your Top 5 list. Share their story with your harvest team.

In the next chapter, you will gain godly wisdom, which will show you how to follow God's lead. Step up and love people with God's love, find the lost, and ignite a movement for people no one has ever reached before.

KEY TAKEAWAYS

- **Jesus' Gut-Wrenching Compassion:** He saw crowds "harassed and helpless, like sheep without a shepherd" (Matthew 9:36)—that's God's heart for the lost, and it must grip yours too, breaking what breaks His.

- **Myth Busted:** Ministry (preaching, programs) matters more than people, but God loves souls above all (1 John 4:8, John 3:16)—shift from church activity to heart-aching pursuit of the adrift.

- **God's Heart in Action:** Name who breaks yours—a people group, immigrants, coworkers—and let it fuel prayer; if it doesn't ache like Jesus' did, stop and ask Him to stir it.

- **Practical Tools:** Discovery Bible Groups for rookies (free, multilingual, question-based on John)—simple, reproducible for Bible newbies to lead, sparking faith without intimidation.

- **Top 5 Names List:** Write five lost people you know, pray daily for their salvation—Pastor Isaac's wife did this, and three came to Christ the next day; praying stirs compassion you can't ignore.

- **The 3 Ls Revisited:** Locate (go to their world), Listen (hear stories without judgment), Love (engage meaningfully)—start one conversation today, turning everyday moments into eternal seeds.

- **Eternal Stakes:** Lostness means eternal separation (hell, Jesus' top topic after money)—it's not popular, but inescapable; let it break your heart, not harden it.

- **Stories of Pursuit:** Pastor Isaac's instant fruit, Suzanne's mom's lesson ("some names never lifted to the throne"), Paul's hikers ("lost and no one's looking")—who are you looking for?

Pause and Act: Who's on your Top 5 Names list? Pray for them now—one sentence each. This week, use the 3 Ls for one conversation: "What's your story?" Share what God does in the conversations you have with me and let's reach them together.

Chapter 12

Tap Into God's Thoughts

"Imitate me, just as I also imitate Christ."
–1 Corinthians 11:1

Jesus didn't just talk about God's Kingdom. Everything about His life was an expression of that Kingdom. He showed us how to love, lead, and reach the lost. Every step, every word was a lesson, and a training manual for us. Chapter 11 lit a fire to love people like Jesus does, and now, we're diving deeper. How do you tap into God's thoughts to guide you, your leadership and the church you are starting/developing?

It's not about theories or warm fuzzies; it's about following Jesus' playbook, seeking His vision, and knowing your calling. I'm challenging you, planter/pastor: Open the Gospels, see what Jesus did, and do it. Let's unpack how Scripture—through Jesus' life, Nehemiah's vision, and your God-given gifts—shows you the way.

The Myth: Scripture's Just for Inspiration

We love Scripture's stories likeJesus healing, teaching, and dying for us. But too many people, even Christian leaders, treat the Bible like a devotional, rather than a blueprint. The myth is that Scripture's just for inspiration. It acts as a feel-good boost to get through the day. But that mindset is selling the Bible short. The Gospels aren't just proof Jesus is great (He is!); they're a training manual for your calling. Jesus didn't waste a word, and neither should you. If you're not imitating Him, you're missing God's thoughts. We've got to stop just admiring Scripture and start doing what Jesus did. God's Word is your guide to plant and pastor His church.

The Gospels: Jesus' Training Manual

My friend John Worcester taught me this, and it's gold: The Gospels are Jesus' training manual (I want to give credit where it's due). Every move Jesus made was a model. Take the demoniac in Mark 5. Jesus rowed across Galilee for one tormented soul, set him free, and rowed back. One life was worth it all.

That's how He loved people. Intentionally and sacrificially. He listened to outcasts, led with humility, and taught with stories. When He said, "Follow Me, and I will make you fishers of men," He meant for you to imitate everything—His compassion and His heart (Matthew 4:19). Galatians 2:20 says, "I have been crucified with Christ; it is no longer I who live, but Christ lives in me." Live His life, Christian leader. The Spirit is ready to empower you to do it. Open Matthew, Mark, Luke, or John today. What's Jesus doing? How is He training you?

Paul got it, saying, "Imitate me, as I imitate Christ" (1 Corinthians 11:1). In the Gospels, Jesus shows you how to pray for the lost (Luke 6:12), confront sin (John 8:11), and disciple rookies (Mark 3:14). Don't just read—*do*. If His thoughts dwell in you richly (Colossians 3:16), you'll pursue people like He did.

Nehemiah's Steps: Building God's Vision

God's thoughts aren't just in the Gospels—they're in His vision for your church. Nehemiah's story (Nehemiah 1-3) shows how to catch and build that vision. Many pastors, teachers, and authors, like Andy Stanley, bestselling author of one of my favorite books, *Visioneering*, and pastor of North Point Community Church in Atlanta, GA, have outlined Nehemiah's process, but let's break down six core steps to guide you.

The Lord of the church has a vision for you—let's find it. Pull out your Bible, or your phone, and open Nehemiah in the Old Testament.

Step 1: Holy Curiosity

Read Nehemiah 1:1-2. Nehemiah started by asking about Jerusalem's condition. You need that divine curiosity just like that. How many are lost and without Christ in your town? Who's unreached? How many churches have closed nearby? For example, the UCC reported 11 church closures in Massachusetts between 2012-2015.[30] What groups, youth, immigrants, and addicts need Jesus most in your neighborhood or community? When I visited Montreal, I learned that only 0.3% of Quebecois followed Christ[31]. It broke my heart. What

---

30   Southern New England Conference of the United Church of Christ, "Many Voices, One Mission: Viability," September 5, 2018, https://www.sneucc.org/blogdetail/11710904.

31   George Barna, "Quebec: Canada's Most Unevangelized Province," Barna Group, 2003, https://www.barna.com/research/quebec-canadas-most-unevangelized-province/.

or who is your holy curiosity about? Ask God to spark it, then dig in. Talk to locals and research your county or community.

Step 2: Grief, Prayer, Fasting

Read Nehemiah 1:3-4. Nehemiah heard Jerusalem's walls were rubble, and his heart broke. He wept, fasted, and prayed. When God shows you need—like child sex trafficking or a forgotten people group, it ought to wreck you. That's good. I felt it in Montreal, grieving and realizing there was only one follower of Jesus (*me*) in a crowd of 300 people! Take your grief to God. Plan

Step 3: Pour Out Your Heart

Read Nehemiah 1:5-11. Nehemiah confessed Israel's sins and begged God to act. Pray, fast, and cry out to God for your community. Let the need drive you to your knees. Pour your heart out—use his prayer as a guide. Swap "Israel" for your concern: "Lord, hear my cry for the 'youth' (use your own word choice) in this city." Ask for success, like Nehemiah did with the king. Who's your "king," from whom do you need favor and assistance? A landlord? The city council? Pray for God to open doors (Matthew 7:7-8).

Step 4: Ask God to Make a Way

Read Nehemiah 1:11-2:5. Nehemiah needed the king's favor— and he took a life-or-death risk. A cupbearer like Nehemiah could be killed for not showing joy in the King's presence. You need God to move mountains—permits, partners, provision. What doors must open for you to reach your people? Name them in prayer. Trust God to pave the way, like He did for Nehemiah.

Step 5: Act on the Vision

Read Nehemiah 2:6-11. Nehemiah got the king's blessing and went to Jerusalem. When God opens doors, obstacles move. Start that Discovery Bible Group, as I discussed in chapter 11). Meet the people on your Top 5 Names list. Don't wait—*act*. Faith steps fuel the vision.

Step 6: Build with Others

Read Nehemiah 2:17-3:32. Nehemiah rallied teams to rebuild. You can't plant alone. Share your vision with your harvest team. Equip them with the *3 Ls* we discussed in chapter 4. God's vision grows through "we," not "me."

These six steps aren't theory—they work. I've seen Christian leaders, including myself, captured by God's vision by reading these chapters in Nehemiah.

Now, as you begin to live this message out and seek people to share your vision, it's important that you find people whose gifts complement yours. But, in order to do that well, you need to first understand your own gifts and calling.

Your Calling and Gifts: APEST

God's thoughts shape your calling, how you lead, and even how organizations and denominations organize their structures. However, it's amazing how this next topic is so overlooked and yet so significant.

Ephesians 4:11-12 lists five gifts—APEST: **A**postle, **P**rophet, **E**vangelist, **S**hepherd, and **T**eacher. Apostles pioneer new works, like church plants. Prophets speak God's truth, calling for change. Evangelists share the Gospel boldly. Shepherds care for souls, nurturing growth. Teachers unpack Scripture, grounding faith. Which resonates with you? Don't label yourself yet. Just ask your team, "What gifts do you see in me?" Certainly, God affirms callings through others. Jeff Christopherson's book, *Once You See*[32], is an excellent resource to understand APEST. I encourage you to read it.

This will help you find the right people—APEST gifted people—for your team, reach the lost (Luke 19:10), and truly begin to see movement (church planting and growth) over dying churches.

A Story of Vision: Montreal's Cry

In Montreal, I saw God's thoughts break through. Back in the early 2000s, only 0.3% of Quebecois knew Jesus—a statistic that hit me like a gut punch. I grieved, fasted, prayed, asking God to make a way for the Gospel to reach these people. Like Nehemiah, I poured out my heart, begging for open doors. We began to do very creative outreaches that helped us reach many people for Christ and many in this very lost people group came to faith. Today, more and more people are finding Christ. That's God's vision in a specific, urgent, and alive way. What's your vision? Let God wreck you for your city, a people, a place, and your Top 5 list.

Your Call to Follow Jesus

It isn't about head knowledge—it's about living Jesus' life. The Gospels show you how; Nehemiah shows you vision; APEST shows your role.

---

32   Jeff Christopherson, Once You See: A Vision for Church Multiplication (Alpharetta, GA: Exponential, 2020), 45-67.

Stop and pray: "Lord, show me Your thoughts. Spark my curiosity, reveal my gifts."

Here are a few ways you can take action immediately.

- Open one of the Gospels (Matthew, Mark, Luke or John) today—read one story. What's Jesus doing? Go do that today.

- Follow Nehemiah's steps—ask one question or even multiple questions about the need or needs in your community.

- Reflect on APEST—talk to a mentor, pastor, or Christian friend about your gifts. Tap into God's thoughts, live like Jesus, and walk with Jesus in building His church.

Live Christ's Life

The Church Planting Pathway is your map, loving people is your fuel, but God's thoughts are your guide. As you're praying over the lost in your community, stories like the demoniac's freedom and Nehemiah's walls show what happens when you follow Jesus' manual. Pray again: "Father, let Christ live in me." This week, imitate Christ and catch God's vision for His church.

Right about now, you may be tempted to skip some of my recommendations so far. You may be thinking that you don't need help, or maybe you don't know where to begin finding the right help. Surely it's easier to just go it alone?

Wrong! In the next chapter, we're going to talk about that very myth. You definitely don't want to try and tackle this alone. No matter how much easier it may seem.

KEY TAKEAWAYS

- **Imitate Christ:** Jesus' life is your training manual (1 Corinthians 11:1)—every step, word, and act a model; don't just read the Gospels, live them, like rowing across Galilee for one soul (Mark 5).

- **Myth Busted:** Scripture's just for inspiration, not action—stop admiring Jesus; start imitating Him, as Paul did, to avoid missing God's blueprint for your plant.

- **Nehemiah's Vision Steps:** Holy Curiosity (ask about your community's lost, Nehemiah 1:1-2); Grief/Prayer/Fasting (let neediness break you, Nehemiah 1:3-4); Pour Out Heart (confess and beg God, Nehemiah 1:5-11); Ask for a Way (pray for open doors, Nehemiah 1:11-2:5); Act on Vision (move when God says go, Nehemiah 2:6-11); Build with Others (rally your team, Nehemiah 2:17-3:32).

- **Montreal's Breakthrough:** Gary's grief over 0.3% believers led to outreaches that sparked faith—your divine curiosity (e.g., child trafficking) will wreck you and open doors.

- **Calling Without Age Limits:** "Don't let anyone look down on you because you're young" (1 Timothy 4:12)—God calls at any age; Ethan's first sermon at 20 shows it's about heart, not years.

- **Gifts: APEST Framework:** Ephesians 4:11-12's Apostle (pioneer), Prophet (truth-speaker), Evangelist (Gospel-sharer), Shepherd (caregiver), Teacher (Scripture-unpacker)—reflect: which resonates? Ask your team for affirmation.

- **Your Call:** Open a Gospel story today—what's Jesus doing? Do it. Follow Nehemiah—ask one question about your lost. Pray for APEST gifts to align your team.

Pause and Act: What's one Nehemiah step you'll take this week (e.g., curiosity question)? Journal about what resonated with you from this chapter.

Chapter 13

God's Thoughts 2.0

*"Without counsel plans fail, but with many
advisers they succeed."*
—Proverbs 15:22

You're all fired up, loving the lost, and tapping into God's vision. But here's a hard truth: Passion alone is not enough. I've been there, thinking my plan was so exciting, only for it to fall flat. We need God's thoughts.

God's thoughts don't just come from Scripture or your heart; they come through godly counsel as well. Proverbs 12:15 warns, "The way of fools seems right to them, but the wise listen to advice." This is one of the church's biggest misses—going solo when God can give us advisors. I'm begging you, planter and pastor: Don't make decisions alone. Let's unpack why godly counsel is critical and how to find it, because your Christ-like leadership depends on it.

The Myth: I Can Do This Alone

As pastors, we love being visionary leaders, calling shots, and chasing dreams. But the myth is that you can plant and lead a church on your own wisdom. That's a trap, and it's quite foolish to fall into the thinking that you can do this in your own wisdom. Proverbs 14:12 says, "There is a way that seems right to a man, but its end is the way to death."

I've seen leaders burn out, fail, or hurt others because they didn't seek counsel. You're not smarter than God's design. He gave the idea of "wise counsel" for a reason. Going solo's not heroic; it's foolish. We risk blowing it when we ignore godly wisdom around us. Shift now and lean on others to hear God's thoughts clearly.

The Power of Godly Counsel

Godly counsel isn't just advice; it's wisdom rooted in Christ. Proverbs 15:22 promises, "Without counsel, plans fail, but with many advisers they succeed." Counsel protects you from blind spots, sharpens your vision, and saves you pain. When I was a young pastor, I learned this the hard way. Counsel's not about slowing you down. Godly advice is about building a team that hears God together. Whether it's your harvest team (chapter 7), a mentor, or a network, wise voices keep you aligned with God's thoughts. Why learn lessons the hard way when the right counsel offers you God's perspective?

A Story of Learning: Fort Worth Fumble

Let me tell you about a time I blew it. As a youth pastor in Fort Worth, Texas, I planned an epic mission trip for my students—location booked, details set, ready to roll. I was pumped, thinking it'd change lives. Then my senior pastor called me in." Gary, I hear you've set up this trip," he said. "Yeah, it's gonna be awesome!" I replied. His face fell." I wish you'd talked to me first." Turns out, the place and pastor I'd chosen to visit had issues I didn't know about, stuff that could've harmed my students, not to mention our church's reputation." Call and cancel," he said. I was embarrassed, a little upset, definitely humbled, but I obeyed.

As I was apologizing for my mistake, he kindly dropped this gem: "Gary, I'd rather ride a bucking bronco than a dead horse." He saw my heart, but he also taught me a lesson: Seek counsel first. I could've learned through pain, taking kids to the wrong place, or through his wisdom. That day, I vowed never to plan big without advisors. It's not weakness; it's God's way. Counsel protects and saves you from costly stumbles.

Finding Godly Counselors

Counsel's only as good as the source. Look for people who walk with Jesus, know His Word, and love the harvest. They're not yes-men; they'll challenge you with truth. Proverbs 11:14 says, "Where there is no guidance, a people falls, but in an abundance of counselors there is safety." Your Pathway team is a start. Even those who are young in their faith can help guide and shape your perspective. I've leaned on men and women who've planted and pastored before, like my Fort Worth pastor. Ask God for these voices; they'll guard you in ways you can't see.

How do you find them? Pray specifically: "Lord, send me wise counselors." Ask your network. Meet with a mentor, advisor, or counselor monthly. Share your plans, big or small, and listen. If they say, "Slow down," trust them. It's not about control; it's about success from God's perspective. Where do you want to learn your lessons—painful mistakes or godly wisdom? Choose the latter.

Your Call to Seek Counsel

This is short and sweet, but don't miss it: God's thoughts come through His Word, His Spirit, and His people. Don't plant and pastor alone—seek counsel to stay sharp. Stop and pray: "Father, send me godly advisors and guard my steps through them." This is why in the church planting pathway, we give advice and counsel every step of the way and as needed. Every Christian leader needs this. You need it. So, seek it out. I'm urging you: find your counselors, hear God's thoughts, and lead with Jesus' mind and heart.

Wisdom for the Harvest

The Church Planting Pathway is your map, loving people is your fuel, God's vision is your guide, but counsel is your guardrail. My Fort Worth fumble taught me: solo plans fail, but wisdom born from counsel wins. Pray again: "Lord, surround me with Your counsel."

Find one advisor this week and call them to share your heart. The lost are waiting, Jesus' manual is open, and counsel keeps you steady and prevents you from doing foolish things. Step up, Christian leader. Listen to God's people, align with His thoughts, and build a church that lasts—one that is built with Jesus leading the way.

This was a short but oh so necessary chapter. It's imperative that you are walking in wisdom, godly counsel, and obedience!

We're heading into the final chapter, where we begin putting everything together. And I've asked my wife, Sue, to weigh in with her thoughts. She is such a gifted encourager!

KEY TAKEAWAYS

- **Myth Busted:** You can plant and lead alone, but Proverbs 14:12 warns, "there is a way that seems right to a man, but its end is death"—solo wisdom leads to failure; godly counsel is God's design for success.

- **Counsel's Power:** Proverbs 15:22 promises, "without counsel plans fail, but with many advisers they succeed." Wise voices protect blind spots, sharpen vision, and save pain, turning potential stumbles into breakthroughs.

- **Fort Worth Fumble:** My mishap as a youth pastor—planning a mission trip without input, only to learn from his senior pastor's "bucking bronco vs. dead horse" wisdom—shows counsel prevents costly mistakes.

- **Seek the Right Voices:** Look for Christ-followers who know Scripture and love the harvest—not yes-men, but truth-speakers (Proverbs 11:14); pray specifically for them, as they guard what you can't see.

- **Practical Pursuit:** Meet a counselor monthly, share your plans big or small, and listen—even if it's "slow down"—it's not control, it's God's way to multiply your impact.

- **Church Planting Tie-In:** The Pathway's Advice/Counsel element ensures personalized wisdom every step, abundant and accessible, unlike scarce coaching—tap it to stay aligned with Jesus' mission.

Pause and Act: What decision are you facing alone right now? Pray Proverbs 15:22 and name one counselor to contact this week—share your plan and ask, "What am I missing?"

Chapter 14

Know Your Purpose

"For we are His workmanship, created in Christ Jesus for good works, which God prepared beforehand, that we should walk in them."
–Ephesians 2:10

I asked my wife, Sue, to share from her heart in this chapter about purpose. She passionately loves Jesus. She has so many talents. Certainly, God has gifted her to be a great team builder. She has a huge heart for ministry, for serving people and helping them find their place in God's purpose for their lives. You will be enriched as you listen to her.

She and I have been married for thirty-one years, and she has been the main "discipler" in our kids' lives. She currently works part-time in building relationships and sharing the Gospel with master's level international students in Boston, MA, and she serves part-time as my administrator with Alliance New England.

Sue's Perspective

I'm Sue, Gary's wife, and for decades we've poured our hearts into planting churches and mentoring believers to shine for Jesus. Gary's fire for the lost drives him to preach and plant; my passion is walking alongside people, new believers, planters, or quiet attendees, to discover their God-given purpose. He asked me to share my perspective in this chapter because I've seen the harvest transform when everyone, not just pastors, steps into their role. I met a woman, hesitant to serve, who found her calling leading outreach after we explored her gifts together.

That's my heart: helping you and those you lead find your unique design to reach souls. You're God's workmanship, crafted for His work.

I've watched countless people—new believers, faithful attendees, church planters—wonder, "What's my purpose?" Maybe you're leading a ministry, planning an outreach, or planting a church among the unchurched. Maybe you're longing to see those you lead catch fire for God's harvest.

The Potter (Isaiah 64:8) designed you to shine (Matthew 5:14-16), and I'm thrilled to help you find that. Let's unpack how every believer can live their purpose, because the harvest needs us all.

The Myth: Ministry Is Only for Pastors

Here's a myth we've got to bust: Ministry is only for pastors or church planters. Those trained for service. Too many churches lean on only one leader to preach, pray, and reach the lost, while church attenders sit in the pews, unengaged. That's not

God's design for ministry, and it's failing us. Ephesians 4:12 says pastors equip "the saints for the work of ministry." Gary's always saying, "The pastor's job is to equip the people—they've been made with a purpose in God's Kingdom!" We're in a crisis of co-laborers (Luke 10:2); the harvest is waiting because we think only the "called" leaders can, or should, serve. But that's wrong.

Every believer's called to proclaim the Gospel in one way or another. For some, their calling is church planting or pastoring (you should consider this seriously and seek God's desire for you in this before just saying, "this is not me." For others, their calling might be about stewarding their resources or serving quietly behind the scenes. You're designed for impact, not the sidelines. Let's shift that thinking: Your church will thrive when everyone knows their purpose.

Your Unique Design: SHAPE

God's heart is to shape you for His harvest. As a mentor, I love guiding people to discover their purpose through what Rick Warren calls **SHAPE**—Spiritual Gifts, Heart (your passions), Abilities, Personality, and Experiences—in his book, *The Purpose Driven Church*[33].

Your **SHAPE** reveals how God's wired you to build His church (1 Corinthians 12:4-31). We've modified Rick Warren's teaching, over the years, and we've seen it transform lives. Let's walk through each, so you can equip others, or yourself, to experience God's plan for kingdom impact.

---

33   Rick Warren, The Purpose Driven Life: What on Earth Am I Here For? (Grand Rapids, MI: Zondervan, 2002), 233-34.

1. **Spiritual Gifts: What Has the Holy Spirit Gifted You to Do?**

   1 Corinthians 12:4-7 says, "There are different kinds of gifts, but the same Spirit distributes them… for the common good." 1 Peter 4:10 adds, "Each of you should use whatever gift you have received to serve others." Are you gifted to teach, serve, encourage, or lead? Maybe you're an evangelist. Ask God to reveal your gifts, then try them. Facilitate a Discovery Bible Group or pray for your Top 5 Names list. I've seen shy believers discover they're gifted to intercede, changing lives through prayer. I've seen others erupt in enthusiasm when they realized God had gifted them in special and unique ways. There is such a special joy for people when they realize the Spirit has gifted them to fulfill God's purposes!

2. **Heart: What Do You Love to Do?**

   Philippians 2:13 says, "It is God who works in you to will and to act in order to fulfill His good purpose." What fires you up? Kids? Refugees? Justice? Gary's heart breaks for the lost and to find leaders who will reach them; mine aches to mobilize people to serve. Your passions point to your purpose. Ask, "Who do I care about? What keeps me up at night?" Write it down and then act on it. If you love youth, locate young people, listen to them, love them, and start to share Jesus with them (the 3 Ls). Your heart's desires are a clue to God's calling and purposes for you.

3. **Abilities: What Skills Can You Offer?**

   Exodus 31:3 describes God filling artisans with "skill, ability, and knowledge." Ecclesiastes 9:10 urges,

"Whatever your hand finds to do, do it with all your might." Your talents—writing, organizing, coding, cooking—are tools for the harvest. I've seen accountants steward church funds, musicians lead worship, and teachers disciple new believers. List your skills, then ask, "How can I use these for Jesus?" No ability is too small. God can use it all (1 Corinthians 10:31).

4. **Personality: Who Are You?**

Psalm 139:13-16 says God knit you together, fearfully and wonderfully. Are you outgoing or reflective? Analytical or creative? Your personality shapes your ministry. Gary's bold: He loves preaching to crowds. I'm extroverted, thriving in groups and gatherings of all sizes. All types of people, shy or outgoing, are useful in the Body of Christ. Reflect: "What traits describe me?" Then lean in. Introverts make great listeners for the lost; extroverts rally teams. Your wiring is no accident.

5. **Experiences: What's Shaped You?**

2 Corinthians 1:3-4 says God comforts us so we can comfort others. Your life—joys, pains, triumphs, failures—equips you to serve. I've walked through loss, which lets me empathize with hurting women. Gary's experience in watching and walking with multiple church planters and pastors fuels his passion to advise others. What's molded you? A divorce? A mission trip? Share your story, like Paul did (1 Thessalonians 2:8). Your past is God's training ground for impact.

SHAPE: Spiritual Gifts, Heart, Abilities, Personality, and Experiences. These aspects of Rick Warren's framework show us that the aspects of ourselves aren't just for us. . They are for those you *lead*, too. Disciple someone through these questions: "What's your gift? Your passion?" I've seen unengaged church attendees light up when they find their role and become investors, not just attendees. God's designed you, and your people, for His harvest and a unique purpose.

Serving God's Purpose in This Generation

Gary's life verse, Acts 13:36, drives us as a family: "When David had *served God's purpose in his own generation*, he fell asleep." Acts 20:24 adds, "My only aim is to finish the race and complete the task the Lord Jesus has given me—the task of testifying to God's grace." We're called to serve our generation. I challenge you to make Acts 13:36 your life verse too and commit to serving God's purpose.

God placed this book in your hands. The church in North America is in a crisis, and it's time for you to step up! It's time for you to challenge your people to step up.

As the book, *The Best Kept Secret of Christian Missions* by John Dickson[34], says, "everyone is called to proclaim the Gospel—whether they are a pastor or not." And it also says, "everyone is uniquely gifted to play their part in sharing the Gospel with whatever giftedness God's Spirit has given them." Call people to this message.

Matthew 28:18-20 commands us to make disciples, yet many sit back, leaving pastors to burn out. But many of those "sitting

---

34   John Dickson, The Best Kept Secret of Christian Missions: Recovering the Notion that Every Christian Is a Missionary (Waynesboro, GA: Paternoster, 2002), 15-20.

back" would step into the work of God's kingdom if they were asked, if they knew they were to have this as their main purpose, and if they knew they were needed. Do your people know they are needed?

The Church Planting Pathway shows us that ministry is a team effort. Do you believe in APEST? Do you believe that God has provided Apostles, Prophets, Evangelists, Shepherds, and Teachers for His church? Then mobilize apostles to pioneer, shepherds to care, and evangelists to share. Raise up leaders and pray for the Lord of the harvest to send them to you (Matthew 9:38).

I've seen Gary coach new believers into passionate, gifted church planters and pastors, while I've mentored many into ministry and their gifting. God's saying, "You might not feel called to pastor, but what about starting something? Serving somewhere?" Pray, "Lord, who's my co-laborer?" The harvest waits.

A Story of Purpose: Our Journey

Where Gary's skills and gifts are in vision casting, equipping, preaching, planting and revitalizing churches, and sharing the Gospel, I'm more likely to be planning events, offering hospitality, and investing in women and volunteers. Together, we've seen God use our SHAPE to build His church. Gary's gift is teaching; mine is encouragement. His passion is church planters and church leaders; mine is volunteers. His skills, vision-casting, and advising complement my listening and mobilizing. Our personalities— his boldness, my calm— balance us.

Our experiences living cross-culturally and raising kids shaped our ministry. Acts 13:36 and 20:24 fuel us to serve God's purpose and finish the race.

Early in our ministry, we met a couple who started a church in their Bloomington, Indiana, home. They weren't pastors—just teachers with a heart for the lost. They discipled a handful, then passed the church to a pastor when it grew beyond their little living room. That's SHAPE in action: They used their gifts (teaching), passion (community), skills (hospitality), personality (welcoming), and experiences (faith) to launch, not lead. It's a model for you—start something, then equip others to carry it.

Your Call to Equip

This is your job: know your purpose and help others find theirs. You're not just planting or pastoring a church—you're equipping saints for Kingdom impact (Matthew 5:14-16). Stop and pray: "Father, show me my SHAPE. Use me to equip others."

Here's your action plan to start putting all of this into immediate practice:

- Reflect on SHAPE: Write answers to the five questions (gifts, passions, abilities, personality, experiences). Share with a mentor.

- Disciple Someone: Pick one person, a new believer or unengaged attendee. Walk them through SHAPE over coffee.

- Mobilize Your Team: Assign roles based on APEST and SHAPE. Need a leader? Raise one up or ask God specifically for them. God's probably prepared them, and they are ready for an ask from you. In step 4 of the Church Planting Pathway, Gary gave advice and counsel to the planter. This will help them raise up a team mobilizer so the weight of team development and training does not fall solely on the church planter.

- Start Something: Launch a Discovery Bible Group and help others to start even more groups. Develop an outreach plan that will make sense and build a bridge into the people of your community. Then begin to implement your plan.

Live Your Purpose

Every person you will ever meet has been created for a purpose. First of all, you. You have an amazing purpose. In a sense, your purpose is to help others find theirs! As Jesus told us in (John 4), there is a vast harvest waiting to find that purpose.

If God's people choose not to find their purpose or help others to find theirs, the church will continue to die! Live this purpose!

KEY TAKEAWAYS

- **Sue's Heart:** As Gary's wife and a mentor, I've shared my passion for helping believers discover their God-given design—equipping new and faithful alike to step into the harvest with purpose (Ephesians 2:10).

- **Myth Busted:** Ministry is only for pastors—Ephesians 4:12 says leaders equip saints for the work; the crisis of co-laborers means everyone's called to proclaim the Gospel, from stewarding resources to serving quietly (Luke 10:2).

- **SHAPE Framework:** God's Potter shapes you (Isaiah 64:8) through Spiritual Gifts (1 Corinthians 12:4-7), Heart/Passions (Philippians 2:13), Abilities (Exodus 31:3), Personality (Psalm 139:13-16), and Experiences (2 Corinthians 1:3-4)—reflect to uncover your unique role.[35]

- **Mobilize the Body:** APEST calls apostles to pioneer, prophets to speak truth, evangelists to share, shepherds to care, teachers to ground—affirm gifts in others to raise co-laborers (Ephesians 4:11-12).

- **Crisis of Calling:** Retirements outpace leaders; start like Suzanne's parents (home church, then pass to a pastor)—launch, don't hoard; pray for workers God's preparing (Matthew 9:38).

- **Our Legacy:** Acts 13:36 ("served God's purpose in his generation") and 20:24 ("finish the race, testify to grace") fuel our planting. Your SHAPE is for eternity's impact.

---

35   Rick Warren, The Purpose Driven Life: What on Earth Am I Here For? (Grand Rapids, MI: Zondervan, 2002), 23.

- **Equip for Impact:** Disciple through SHAPE questions; start outreaches, form teams—God's designed you to build His church, one purpose at a time.

Pause and Act: What's one SHAPE area to explore (e.g., your passion)? Pray Ephesians 2:10: "Show me my good works." This week, ask one person, "What's your gift?" and help them serve.

It's Time to Become Dangerous

*"These men who have turned the world upside
down have come here, too."*
–Acts 17:6

I started the book with stats like these: 135 churches closed their doors this week in the US permanently. Canada has had a sharp decline in Christ-followers. So many more people die annually than those who are coming to Christ in North America.

Is God done with the North American church? Has He decided to move on to other continents and let us become like the Christian church in Turkey or other countries, which once was strong and thriving and now barely exists? Or, would He use someone like you to be a part of a new movement here in North America?

The Lie That Stops Us

Here's the lie we've got to crush: Planting a church or reaching the lost is too hard and only for "special" leaders. That's nonsense. God doesn't need superstars—He needs you, right where you are. You don't need a big budget or a theology degree. You need a heart broken for people, a willingness to follow Jesus' example, wise voices to guide you, and a harvest team ready to serve alongside you. God's designed you for this, whether you're preaching, praying, or opening your home. The harvest is vast, and every believer's called to it. Don't let fear or doubt keep you on the sidelines.

The Heart of It All

Here's the most important thing for you to know: God loves people more than anything—He sent His Son to prove it (John 3:16). That's the fire driving your call.

Jesus saw crowds "harassed and helpless, like sheep without a shepherd" (Matthew 9:36), and His heart broke. Yours should too. He didn't just talk about love; He lived it by eating with sinners, healing outcasts, and dying for us all. Your purpose is the same. It comes back down to the 3 Ls: go **locate** where people are, **listen** to their stories, and **love** them with Jesus' love.

Pray for the lost, share the Gospel simply, and watch God move. It's not about programs—it's about people desperately in need of Jesus.

You've got a clear path: follow Jesus' lead, like He showed in the Gospels, as he crossed a lake for one soul (Mark 5). Seek God's vision, like Nehemiah, who grieved when he found out the need, and then he acted to rebuild (Nehemiah 1:4). Surround yourself with godly advisors, so your plans will not fail (Proverbs 15:22).

Equip everyone around you, from new believers to faithful attendees, to discover their God-given purpose—spiritual gifts, passions, skills, personality, and experiences (Ephesians 2:10). Help as many people as possible to live out God's purposes in this generation (Acts 13:36), and in doing so, the church will have new life and vibrancy again!

Who Are You Looking For?

Remember the story of my friend Paul in the Canadian Rockies? He led tourists, got lost, and realized, "It's one thing to be lost; it's another to be lost and no one's looking for you." That's the world—millions wandering, and too few searching. I'm challenging you: Be the one who *sees* lost people. Your neighbors, coworkers, the stranger at the coffee shop…they're who Jesus died for.

Make a commitment right now to see people differently.

Remember Acts 20:24: "My only aim is to finish the race and complete the task the Lord Jesus has given me—the task of testifying to God's grace." That's your task, too. The harvest needs you *now*.

The dying North American church needs you *now*.

You're designed for this!

Turn the page for **Next Steps**—practical ways to work with me, build your team, and start seeing a resurrected church in North America.

It's time to become dangerous!

With great love and affection,

Gary Smith

Next Steps

My team and I would love to help you launch a brand new church or strengthen your existing one. Here are some quick ways you can dive into more training with me and our team.

First things first: We want to start an initial conversation to consider what you've read and your next steps. Follow this QR code or visit our website:

https://thechurchplantingpathway.com/talkwithgary

As we talk, we can formulate a plan for your next steps. We are excited to talk with you! Excited to see more churches birthed and more church planters strengthened, encouraged, and activated to serve Jesus in the harvest fields! They truly are "white unto harvest" (John 4:35).

And if you're pastoring an existing church, we are excited to walk with you as you refocus and bring your church back to focusing on the work of the harvest.

About the Author

Gary Smith is a passionate catalyst for advancing the Kingdom of God through disciple-making, church planting, and dynamic churches that transform communities. With thirty-seven years of ministry experience across the United States, Canada, and beyond, Gary has served as a pastor, missionary, and church planting leader.

Gary has done Master's Level studies at Southwestern Baptist Theological Seminary, Denver Seminary, and Grace Seminary. His undergraduate degree is from Ottawa University. Today, he serves as Church Planting Director with Alliance New England, Northeast Regional Church Multiplication Coordinator with the Christian and Missionary Alliance, and Senior Master Trainer with Dynamic Church Planting International.

Gary and his wife, Sue, live in Quincy, Massachusetts, and have four grown children who continue the family's legacy of faith and service.